Praise for *A Mindset for S*

Tony Swainston has conducted numerous workshops for teachers and supervisors throughout the Kingdom of Saudi Arabia, all of which have been extremely well-received and have practical applications. *A Mindset for Success* addresses the practical needs of leaders and teachers across a range of educational settings. The motivational approaches to changing mindsets and engaging stakeholders in the educational process are refreshing, innovative and will contribute to improving student outcomes.

Tony's positive and clear approach makes his theories transferable to the classroom. The book provides guidance in the collective teaching and learning engagement approach we are striving to move towards in the Kingdom; encouraging all stakeholders to recognise, realise and action their responsibilities in preparing our children for the future that lies ahead of them.

Abdulrahman Alfuraih, Head of English Language, Ministry of Education, Saudi Arabia

A great insight into the ways in which we can improve outcomes for students. Tony is able to share his passion and belief that through hard work, determination and deliberate practice we can all accomplish much more. Having worked alongside Tony to unpick this principle of growth mindsets, we have seen students and adults change their views and opinions.

It is my belief that, if we get this fundamental principle correct in the classroom, many more of our students will achieve much more and levels of aspiration will significantly increase.

Ian Mottram, Head Teacher, Le Cateau CP School

A must-read and must-do for school leaders who are serious about creating the very best organisational culture and environment for success. Tony takes you straight to the heart of the matter – schools have to be the ultimate role model for changing mindsets. This can only be achieved by leaders, teachers, students and parents, both as individuals and as a collective, being guided to view things through a different lens. With absolute clarity of thought and process, Tony prods and provokes our conscience at all levels and shows us how we can achieve it.

Michael Gernon, CEO and Principal, GEMS Wellington Academy

In schools we are always self-evaluating and looking to improve practice, something which is often driven by data trends and can often lead to much of our improvement work being subject specific. Therefore, as a school leader it is refreshing and energising to focus on how we can improve our practice overall. Tony's book is a reminder not only of why we work in schools but also the impact we can have on children's lives.

A Mindset for Success takes you from theory to practice in a very pragmatic way. From his initial exploration of the work of the theorists, right through to the practical application in the classroom, Tony's narrative is clear, accessible and engaging. Tony deeply believes that mindsets matter: his passion for developing mindsets for success makes a positive difference not only to the children we teach but also to ourselves as teachers, the people responsible for preparing children for the challenges of their lives ahead. This is evident throughout the book and in our experience working with Tony at our school in Ripon.

Paul Bowlas, Head Teacher, Holy Trinity CE Junior School

How do we create a school culture in which students feel confident and achieve success? Founded on years of teaching, observation, reading and coaching, Tony's excellent book lays out a clear and compelling case for developing growth mindsets in schools. Teachers and leaders should enjoy the clarity of exposition, the practical usefulness of the ideas and Tony's sheer passion for the subject.

Tony demonstrates how coaching and deliberate practice can change a school culture, providing practical ideas for communicating a growth mindset to teachers and pupils. Drawing on the work of scholars such as Hattie, Dweck, Seligman and Ericsson, Tony explains how the brain works and how we can develop motivation, resilience, grit, perseverance and well-being in students.

Leaders will welcome the analysis of how best to effect change in schools, in particular the value of the drip-feed approach to change management, including not only teachers, but parents, support staff and governors. Teachers will value Tony's specific ideas for carrying out action research in this field.

There is no doubt that the beliefs and expectations of both students and teachers play a huge role in determining outcomes in schools. Tony develops a very persuasive argument for how changing mindsets can tap into the tremendous potential every person has.

Steve Smith, former head of MFL, author of the forthcoming
Becoming an Outstanding Languages Teacher

A Mindset for Success

Determination

Perseverance

Attitudes

Learning

Values

Resilience

Expectations

Grit

Habits

Beliefs

A Mindset for Success

In Your Classroom and School

Tony Swainston

Crown House Publishing Limited
www.crownhouse.co.uk

First published by
Crown House Publishing Ltd
Crown Buildings, Bancyfelin, Carmarthen, Wales, SA33 5ND, UK
www.crownhouse.co.uk

and

Crown House Publishing Company LLC
PO Box 2223, Williston, VT 05495, USA
www.crownhousepublishing.com

British Library Cataloguing-in-Publication Data

A catalogue entry for this book is available from the British Library.

Print ISBN 978-178583197-3
Mobi ISBN 978-178583227-7
ePub ISBN 978-178583228-4
ePDF ISBN 978-178583229-1

LCCN 2017933993

Printed and bound in the UK by TJ International, Padstow, Cornwall

Acknowledgements

Although this book is not modelled on the OMP (Osiris Mindsets Programme) which has been wonderfully designed by Barry Hymer and substantially developed by Elizabeth Dawson, my experience as an OMP trainer has added to the expertise which I am able to bring to this work. I am enormously indebted to Barry Hymer for the generous way in which he has shared with me and many others his knowledge about mindsets, as well as the insightful way in which he models how to bring great clarity to so many important aspects of impactful classroom and school practice.

Contents

Introduction

I have come to a frightening conclusion. I am the decisive element in the classroom. It is my personal approach that creates the climate. It is my daily mood that makes the weather. As a teacher I possess tremendous power to make a child's life miserable or joyous. I can be a tool of torture or an instrument of inspiration. I can humiliate or humor, hurt or heal. In all situations it is my response that decides whether a crisis will be escalated or de-escalated, and a child humanized or dehumanized.

Haim Ginott[1]

If our schools are to truly bring about the kind of advances that are both desired and required by the changing world that we live in (and that our children will inhabit in the future) then things must change. And a critical part of that change is for schools to move away from many of the talent and IQ myths that presently exist. Schools must stop categorising students in a way that damages their ability to grow and develop. I am not in any way suggesting that schools do this deliberately, but it happens nevertheless, and it is crippling the prospects of many young people to achieve their potential. No matter how well intentioned it may be, classifying certain children as G&T (gifted and talented) or SEN (special educational needs) and perhaps the bulk of children as RHINOs (really here in name only – maybe this is a new acronym for you to add to your growing list of educational acronyms!) can be extremely dangerous. (RHINOs are the group of children who don't create any fuss. They are neither viewed as being the exceptionally gifted or talented students, nor the students who are judged to have SEN issues or are behaviourally challenging.)

There is research, for example, which shows that '88% of children placed in sets or streams at age 4 remain in the same groupings until they leave school'.[2] It is shocking to think that by the time children are 4 years old they might be put into a box of ultimate predetermined achievement, decided for them by other people, and from which they will very likely not escape during their school life. This

---

1   H. G. Ginott, *Teacher and Child: A Book for Parents and Teachers* (New York: Macmillan, 1972), p. 15.
2   A. Dixon, Editorial, *FORUM*, 44(1) (2002), 1.

is particularly disturbing when we all know that children develop at very different rates. If a child is placed into a 'low group' then it is difficult for them to overcome their own belief, and the beliefs of others, that they will never achieve a great deal. They might be presented with less demanding, less satisfying and less stimulating work by sometimes less qualified and lower skilled teachers. The only time they might have the chance to socialise with children from the higher groups may be during breaks away from the set curriculum being delivered in the school. Schools around the UK assert that they are committed to developing the potential inside each child, while at the same time there are customs and practices, like streaming and setting, which actively act against this.

The so-called level of intelligence of students has become so much part of what schools explicitly or implicitly seek to establish that it is likely to take some time to alter this culture. It is all too easy for us to stay with the old ways of assessing students and providing them with unhelpful feedback. It is easy to assess what we presently assess. Our laziness is hidden by references to 'hard data' concerning students which gives us the impression that this is the stuff that really matters. However, we should be reminded that 'Not everything that can be counted counts, and not everything that counts can be counted' (this quote is often attributed to Albert Einstein, although it may have been William Bruce Cameron who first said it), instead of continuing to blindly promote a system that doesn't fit the requirements of the 21st century. The broad bands of uniformity and crude segregation that schools once tried to fit students into, in order to accommodate the industrial world, no longer match the requirements of today's society. And it is not just the very obvious and blatant structures of inequality in educational opportunity on offer to different children that we should be concerned about. It is also the subconscious processes that go on in our schools which present an equally challenging danger for all of us. It may be hard for many of us to leave behind old ways of talking about students, including references to them being 'intelligent' and 'talented' (or otherwise!).

To illustrate how so much that is going on in our subconscious mind radiates out from us to the students, I will describe an experiment carried out by Robert Rosenthal back in 1968.[3] I will tell the story in my own words, which is how I

---

3   R. Rosenthal and L. Jacobson, *Pygmalion in the Classroom: Teacher Expectation and Pupils' Intellectual Development* (New York: Holt, Rinehart and Winston, 1968), see esp. p. 61.

explain it to the audiences I work with, and let you research more about this if you decide to do so. Rosenthal and his research colleague, Lenore Jacobson, devised an IQ test that was given to students in an elementary school, the results of which were analysed by the two researchers. From these investigations, the teachers who would be taking the classes the following year were informed that around 20% of the students had an 'unusual potential for intellectual growth'. These were the students who could be considered the so-called 'intellectual bloomers' in the coming year. The teachers were asked not to indicate to any of the students what the test had shown. Then the researchers left the teachers to get on with their teaching until they came back at the end of the year to give the students the same IQ test. These test results were compared with the first test results and it was found that there was a surprising correlation between the predicted 'bloomers' and the children who had done particularly well that year.

I try to imagine what the conversation may have been like between the researchers and teachers when they sat down to discuss the findings. It may have gone something like this.

> Rosenthal: You know, these results are astonishing.
>
> Teacher A: Why? You knew from your original test that certain students were going to do particularly well. In fact, you told me the names of the 20% of the students who were going to do well. So why is it now such a surprise to you?
>
> Rosenthal: Well, the truth is that we chose the 20% students that we said would do well completely at random. We had no idea who the so-called 'bloomers' might be.

Oops! We can only guess at the sense of surprise, and perhaps a little bit of annoyance, that the teacher would have felt in realising that she had been given false information. Even more surprising for her may have been the fact that the students whom she had been told would be 'bloomers' turned out to be the students who did very well in her class. This is an example of a self-fulfilling prophecy. What the teacher thought about the students had a significant impact on how they performed that year: the students that the teacher thought would do particularly well did do well.

This phenomenon is called the Pygmalion effect. It describes the finding that how a teacher perceives a student will have a very powerful impact on how they develop. And this does not just apply to teachers and students; it happens in the families of the students we teach as well, with parents being very powerful 'Pygmalions' to their children. We might summarise this phenomenon as when we expect certain behaviours from another person, it is very likely that we ourselves will behave in such a way as to make their expected behaviours ever more likely to manifest themselves.

When I have told teachers about the Rosenthal experiment their response is often that the teachers in the experiment can't have been very good, otherwise they would not have been influenced by the information they were given. My understanding is that the teachers chosen for the experiment were in fact good professionals, but they had no idea that they were influencing the children in their classes to succeed in different ways. In fact, just like you or I, they were convinced that they treated all students in a fair way. The truth is that once we accept information we have been given as being a reflection of the truth, then it is very difficult for us not to act on this information, and much of our acting is going on at a subconscious level. Key messages that we are giving out as educators are not always transmitted through the words we speak. In fact, research by Albert Mehrabian indicates that in face-to-face communication the degree to which we decide we like somebody, for example, is influenced only to a small extent by the words spoken.[4] In terms of percentages, it was found that 7% of the signals we receive that influence whether we like another person is through their words, 38% is through the way they speak these words (including tone, intonation and volume) and the other 55% is through their body language (including facial gestures). This gives us an idea about the way that many of the other thoughts and attitudes we have about the students in our classes will manifest themselves beyond the words we speak.

The psychological concept of 'thin-slicing' describes how in a very short period of time, usually less than five minutes, it is possible to draw very accurate conclusions concerning the emotions and attitudes of people interacting with each other. When defining the thin slice, I usually draw on the analogy of a stick of rock, let's say from Blackpool, and with the word 'Blackpool' written inside. If we were to take a sharp knife and cut very thin slices from the rock, each one would have the word Blackpool written on it. In a similar way, from very short interactions – or

---

4   A. Mehrabian, *Silent Messages: Implicit Communication of Emotions and Attitudes* (Belmont, CA: Wadsworth, 1981).

thin slices – we pick up essential information from another person that enables us to make an assessment about them. It lets us know their central message – and whether they are from Blackpool or Whitby!

Pupils, therefore, pick up a thin slice of who their teacher is from their behaviour. This includes the beliefs that the teacher has about each and every one of them as individuals. If a teacher thinks about a particular pupil, 'You are intelligent', then this pupil will thin slice this message without a word being spoken by the teacher. The corollary is that there will be other pupils that the teacher will believe are not quite as intelligent, talented or full of potential, and they will thin slice a very different message which tells them that this teacher thinks they are not intelligent, not gifted, slow, lacking in ability, lacking in potential and so on.

Some teachers have said to me that the experiment carried out by Rosenthal was morally wrong because the teachers were provided with information that was incorrect. Some teachers have also observed that if the school which their own child attends were to carry out an experiment like this then they would be very annoyed, particularly if their child was not one of those randomly chosen to be a 'bloomer'. The reason they give is that their child might be disadvantaged because the teacher does not have a high opinion about their ability to develop during the coming year. And, of course, I can understand this. But at the same time, all of us in education need to take into consideration the high levels of data collection and tracking of students that is going on every day in our schools.

We might need to ask ourselves some of the following questions.

- Is the information and data in our schools helping our students to achieve their full potential? (It is often argued that our schools are now information rich but knowledge poor.)

- Is the information and data in our schools building glass ceilings that limit the full development of the potential that lies inside each student?

- Is the information and data in our schools, which we sometimes pass on to the students themselves, creating self-fulfilling prophecies in their minds?

- Is the information and data in our schools unintentionally encouraging students to take on a fixed mindset?

- Is the information and data in our schools encouraging teachers and other adults in the school to take on a fixed mindset?

- Is the information and data in our schools creating a lot of Pygmalion teachers who actively, although unintentionally, support the development of certain students but at the same time negatively impact upon the development of other students?

Whatever the answer to these questions might be, and if we can't or don't want to change the present requirement for us to collect data, then we can at the very least move towards a mindset for success approach that encourages every child to take on responsibility for their own development. At the same time, each of us as educators can support them through the beliefs that we have about their true potential to achieve amazing results.

We need to remind ourselves that when we stand in front of students and communicate with them they are picking up a thin slice from us which communicates many different things. It might be a frightening thought, but we need to be aware that all students have the equivalent of a PhD in applied psychology when it comes to their ability to interpret the underlying meaning from this thin slice. They are the equivalent in the world of tennis to Venus and Serena Williams and Andy Murray. They have intuitive classroom insights that enable them to read the game of education in a similar way to how Lionel Messi and Mia Hamm read the game of football. They instinctively sense patterns in the classroom. The thin slice of us that they take contains clear indicators of all our beliefs, habits, attitudes and expectations about them, and they sense this almost instantaneously. They don't just 'see right through us' as teachers, they also pick up all the messages that 'radiate out from us' and which provide the building blocks of how we think.

Two themes run throughout this book. These are that (1) the beliefs of students are of crucial importance to their learning, and (2) the potential for achievement and success, which each of us possess through the impressive capacity of our brains, is enormous and largely unknowable. For the purpose of this book I have used the terms 'pupils', 'students' and 'children' in an interchangeable way to refer to the body of young people in our schools who we have the pleasure to see develop and flourish before our eyes. At times, I may also refer to teachers, support staff, classroom support assistants, educators and adults in a similarly interchangeable way. We are all the people who seek to support the development of the young people in our care, and the content of this book is relevant to each and every one of us, no matter what our particular role might be.

Now let us start on a journey into the world of mindsets and learn how we can move towards a mindset for success in our schools.

Part I

Why changing mindsets in our schools matters

Chapter 1

The academic and social impact of mindsets

Whether you believe you can do a thing or not, you are right.

Anon.

Mindsets and academic progress

Professor Carol Dweck, in her remarkable book *Mindset*, provides many examples of where children with a growth mindset academically outperform those children with a fixed mindset.[1]

As we will explore in more detail later on, one such example looked at a group of American students who all had the same maths score when they left elementary school to enter junior high school. (In the UK this would be students leaving junior school to go to secondary school at 11 years of age.) The students were assessed in terms of their mindset: some of them had more of a fixed mindset and others had more of a growth mindset. The students were tracked over a two year period to see how their maths scores changed. The findings showed clearly that the maths scores of the students with a fixed mindset went down, whereas the scores for the students with a growth mindset progressively rose. We will return to what growth and fixed mindsets mean in more detail in Chapter 2.

From my own experience, I too have found that working with schools on a mindset for success programme has brought about significant academic change. For example, a school in Ripon in north Yorkshire that I worked with found that at the end of one year of focusing on mindsets, the academic results were the best the

....

1   C. S. Dweck, *Mindset: The New Psychology of Success* (New York: Random House, 2006).

school had ever had. Of course, it is notoriously difficult to measure the impact of individual interventions in schools. There are so many variables that come into play that it is difficult to draw firm conclusions about what particular intervention has created any change that takes place. The mindset of this head teacher, with his readiness to take a risk on trying something new, being open to possibilities, believing in the potential within each of his staff, as well as the pupils, and having a willingness to find solutions that come from strategies that may not be the most obvious ones, inevitably contributed to the success of the school. However, the head teacher is also convinced that the mindsets intervention was a significant factor in raising the level of attainment in the school. In addition to the academic progress of the pupils, the head teacher reported that both adults and pupils were talking about learning in a very different way at the end of the mindset for success programme than they were at the beginning.

I believe that the two things are in fact interconnected, with the change in language about learning impacting on learning and attainment levels. Although it is far easier to measure changes in something like examination results compared to changes in the beliefs and attitudes of adults and pupils, the latter are nevertheless critically important. There is, obviously, an ongoing and vigorous debate about whether the things that we measure or count in schools, such as examination results, are in fact the things we should focus so much of our attention on in the 21st century. Research clearly indicates that, for example, emotional intelligence (EI) seems to play a far bigger part in the level of success an individual experiences in life compared to the part that IQ plays.[2] Is the main reason that our focus is on IQ in schools because EQ is harder to assess than IQ? Once again, we are reminded of the maxim mentioned earlier on – 'Not everything that can be counted counts, and not everything that counts can be counted' – and how this suggests that we are often drawn to the easier alternative, even though it may not be giving us the best results.

The evidence clearly shows that the type of mindset that a child has will impact on their academic progress, but there is more.

....

2   See, for example, D. Rosete and J. Ciarrochi, Emotional intelligence and its relationship to workplace performance outcomes of leadership effectiveness, *Leadership and Organization Development Journal*, 26 (2005), 388–399.

Mindsets impacting on the social development of pupils

Schools are clearly, and rightly, concerned with providing the best learning for their students. Better academic outcomes for students will enable them to have more options in their lives. But I also know, from personal experience, that teachers, head teachers, support staff, parents and everyone else involved in the nurturing of young people in our schools also care enormously about developing what we might call the 'holistic child'. This is why it is important that, as they progress through and eventually leave school, children are given the tools to support them to face life's challenges and to show determination, grit, resilience and perseverance. These things, which they can learn and develop, will help them to get the most from their lives. Significant in all of this is for children to learn about mindsets and how adopting more of a growth mindset will help them to develop their determination, grit, resilience and perseverance.

In Chapter 4 we will look at the meta-research (research of the research) carried out by Professor John Hattie, which examined a wide range of influences that impact upon the learning of students. His investigation revealed that the most significant thing we can work on as educators, and which makes the biggest difference to the learning of students, is the expectations of the student. Think for a moment about all of the things you could do to support the learning of your students in the classroom. Out of all of these, Hattie has found that it is student expectations (with an effect size of 1.44 for those of you who would like to know this) that comes out as being the most important. And this resonates perfectly, as we shall see, with the findings of Carol Dweck on mindsets. In addition, Hattie found that interventions like social skills programmes, not generally associated directly with academic progress, do in fact support learning in all subjects. This indicates again that enabling and encouraging students to understand more about themselves and others provides them with a better chance of learning well in academic subjects. There is a direct correlation between personal and social development and academic success; in other words, increased levels of EI (which we will look at in more detail in Chapter 8) will support a student's academic progress.

Growth mindsets offer an optimistic view about what is achievable in life for each and every student. But at this point we might want to ask ourselves how much we personally believe that it is possible for people to change the way they view life. For example, how much of our optimism or pessimism is changeable? Well, according to research by psychologist Sonja Lyubomirsky it seems that half of a person's baseline level of well-being comes from their DNA.[3] This baseline level indicates how much we lean towards either cheerfulness or negativity. But, as Donna Wilson says, this leaves plenty of room for each of us to influence our level of optimism through three easy steps.[4]

These three steps involve thoughts, behaviours and brain chemistry, and they help students to improve their feelings and well-being. The following summary provides a little more information about these steps.

1. **Thoughts.** In Chapter 7 we will explore the TEA-R model and how our thoughts affect our emotions, which in turn affect our actions and results. Essentially we are what we think, and students should be taught this in school. We can learn to think in ways that enhance our level of optimism, and the work on mindsets will definitely support this.

2. **Behaviours.** In order to achieve things in life we have to *do* something. Thought itself is not enough. Positive actions and determination will help us to achieve a great deal and alter our level of optimism. In terms of learning, a student needs to know where they are with their learning now, where they want to get to and the next step (or steps) they need to take in order to get there. As educators, it is important that we can provide them with this information and also with the skills they need in order to make the transition. This constant movement towards higher levels of mastery will again encourage the student to have a more optimistic outlook.

3. **Brain chemistry.** The brain produces chemicals called neurotransmitters that affect how we feel. The chemicals that are associated with making us

....

3   S. Lyubomirsky, K. Sheldon and D. Schkade, Pursuing happiness: the architecture of sustainable change, *Review of General Psychology*, 9(2) (2005), 111–131.

4   D. Wilson with M. Conyers, Positive brains are smarter brains, *Edutopia* (9 December 2015). Available at: http://www.edutopia.org/blog/positive-brains-are-smarter-brains-donna-wilson-marcus-conyers.

feel good and creating a positive mood include dopamine, serotonin and oxytocin. One way of producing these chemicals is through physical activity. Therefore, it is wise to tell children that if they are feeling less positive, then some form of physical exercise may well help them to feel a lot better. This message will clearly help them throughout their entire lives, and these 'good mood' chemicals will support them to focus more clearly on the academic work they are doing.

Expanding on the first of these steps, and as a way of helping students to think effectively about their own thinking, I have developed a simple metacognitive model which I use with schools called FACT. F stands for *focus* control, A stands for *advice* control, C stands for *centred* control and T stands for *thought* control.

F Focus control		A Advice control
	FACT Supporting the thinking of children every day	
T Thought control		C Centred control

Focus control

Focus control is about accepting that we have a choice about what we decide to focus our attention on. For example, do we focus on our strengths or our weaknesses? Do we focus on our successes or our failures? Whatever we decide to focus on is our choice, but we must accept that this will influence where we direct our energies. And, of course, once we decide what our main focus of attention is, then our reticular activating system (RAS) will direct our subconscious to be on the lookout for things that correspond to this focus.

(The RAS is something that is very important for us all to know about, and will be explained in Chapter 5.) Teachers who are focused on the 'bad' behaviour of students will see this everywhere, whereas teachers who understand that students can sometimes be challenging but nevertheless also have a lot of very positive characteristics will see examples of students displaying these things all around the school.

Perceptions rule and create our reality for us. We have all come across those people who are doubters or cynics and who want us to prove to them that something is possible. They may say to us, 'Show me and then I'll believe it,' and this is often said with a high degree of self-assurance that sometimes verges on arrogance. In a way, they are saying 'seeing is believing', and if they don't see it then they won't believe it. In my training, I often say to people that 'seeing is believing' is not always true, and that 'believing is seeing' is more in alignment with the way we operate as human beings. Two people may witness the same thing and yet they often see, or experience, wildly different events. As a playful way of illustrating this, I often flash up a PowerPoint slide of the following 20 letters, which is just a series of words without the gaps between them. Before I show them the slide, I ask them to feel free to shout out the words they see as soon as they become apparent. Try this out yourself.

opportunityisnowhere

Okay. What did you first see? Was it 'opportunity is nowhere' or 'opportunity is now here'? I see this as a metaphor for the way we experience the world (though, to be clear, if you happened to read this as 'opportunity is nowhere' I am in no way suggesting that you might have a tendency towards a glass-half-empty approach to life). The point is that we all interpret what we experience around us each and every day, and most of this is happening subconsciously. Some people walk around with an 'opportunity is nowhere' frame of mind, and, surprise, surprise, they wouldn't recognise an opportunity if it came and hit them right between the eyes. Other people walk around with an 'opportunity is now here' frame of mind, and they will be what the 'opportunity is nowhere' folks may call the lucky ones. They find new opportunities around every corner.

If you want to experience for yourself how it is possible to look at something and not see it then you may want to take a break here and look at a video by Daniel

Simons and Christopher Chabris called 'Selective attention test'.[5] In addition, you may like to watch another video about Richard Wiseman's work called 'The luck factor'.[6] This clip demonstrates how it is not so much life events that determine our sense of happiness, positivity and how we describe ourselves as being lucky or unlucky, but rather the way we frame our mind to interpret things.

Focus control therefore reminds us that we must be careful about what we decide to focus on. This is why it is so important for us to have clarity about our goals. With clarity about where we are trying to get to and what we want to achieve, we will be constantly on the lookout for things that support us to achieve our goals. We will return to this idea in Chapter 5 when we learn about how affirmations can support us in our daily lives, together with further information about how the RAS in our brain operates.

Advice control

Many people accept what they are told by other people in matters of critical importance in their life. They may ask a friend, 'Do you think I should go for this job?' and if the friend says, 'No, you're too old for it,' they might decide not to bother applying. A child might have been told at an early age that they cannot draw, and as a result they never put energy into drawing in school. In fact, they may decide that they hate drawing. Of course, it is important that we listen to what other people say and the advice they might give. But, equally, it is also important that we ultimately decide on which comments offered by other people we wish to accept and therefore effectively store in our brains as the 'truth' through neuron connections. We have more choice and control over the acceptance or otherwise of comments made by other people than many of us would perhaps imagine. We can sanction, accept and absorb some ideas and reject others. We have to be very careful about what we accept because this will influence what we think of as being

....

5 See https://www.youtube.com/watch?v=vJG698U2Mvo. See also D. J. Simons and C. F. Chabris, Gorillas in our midst: sustained inattentional blindness for dynamic events, *Perception*, 28(9) (1999), 1059–1074.

6 See https://www.youtube.com/watch?v=ojcM76QLt78.

the way we are. So, we can simply ask ourselves the following: is the thing that is being said to me something that is true, helpful and supportive of my growth? This is not about ignoring good advice; in fact, it is quite the opposite. But it is important for us to be mindful concerning the views of others about ourselves that we accept as being true.

Centred control

A very important psychological idea is the locus of control (LOC). This refers to where we believe the ability to make choices and decisions and to take action is centred in any situation. It is about where we believe the control centre lies: is it within us or does it lie outside of us? When we believe the LOC lies inside of us then we are able to take on responsibility for the actions we decide to take. When we believe the LOC lies outside of us then we believe that we cannot influence things. But at the same time we may complain about things that we have no control over, such as the weather (which is a very popular topic of discussion in the UK). Some of us like to moan about things we have no control over because we can disown responsibility. However, people who are successful in life tend to focus on the things that they can influence. In other words, they direct their attention to where the LOC lies inside of them. This is what we should be encouraging our students to do. Indeed, the research carried out by Carol Dweck shows us that those people with growth mindsets are able to do this. They don't blame themselves or other people for things that might not be exactly the way they would like them to be, but rather they look to see how they themselves can change and improve things. Centred control is very much linked with, and an extension of, focus control, in the same way that all elements of FACT are interrelated.

Let us think for a moment about how important the LOC is for us as teachers and educators. For some teachers, no matter what they try, nothing seems to work the way they would like it to. The students don't respond to them or learn in the way that they would like. They may even become disillusioned with teaching. Teachers are often faced with a stark choice: do they continue to teach and hope that things will improve, or do they decide to leave the profession? Many do leave, often in the first three years of their teaching career. Sometimes, it has to be said, this might well be the right move for everyone involved. Neither teachers nor students will be happy in a classroom that is not filled with optimism, positivity and energy. However, a lot of great expertise and potential is lost from the teaching profession when teachers leave reluctantly but would prefer to stay and become successful. In some cases, there are teachers who were once successful but now find themselves no longer able to recapture the spirit, passion and confidence they once had as educators. In the worst-case scenario, these teachers might end up simply hanging on in there and blaming the students, the leadership in the school, the government, the world and life in general! Their negative beliefs have become hardwired into their brains and they begin to perceive the world, and in particular the students, in a certain way. You may then hear them saying things like:

> Students don't show respect to me these days the way they once did.
>
> The curriculum keeps changing and I can't keep up with it.
>
> Society has made it impossible for me to teach the way I want to.
>
> The school doesn't help me. I feel I'm on my own.

I have heard these statements spoken by various teachers on occasion, and there may be some validity in them. Certainly, for teachers who believe these things to be true they are absolutely true! But remember that perception rules. They will find evidence all around them to satisfy their personal beliefs. However, all of these beliefs take responsibility for success away from the teachers themselves, resulting in them being what I refer to as 'effect teachers' (as opposed to 'cause teachers').

Effect teachers believe:

- The LOC lies outside of me.
- My success is determined by external factors.
- I control very little.
- My self-efficacy is low.

Cause teachers believe:

- The LOC lies within me.
- My success is determined by me.
- I am in control.
- My self-efficacy is high.

A teacher may complain about things that lie outside of his control, as he sees it, such as the level of resources available to him in the classroom. Another teacher may complain about the behaviour of students and say that he has no influence over them anymore because there are factors that he just cannot control. Whether this is true or not is largely irrelevant because if the teacher believes such things then he will act upon them as if they are real. As we shall see, this is directly linked to Dweck's notion of mindsets, with the 'cause teachers' displaying a growth mindset and the 'effect teachers' displaying a fixed mindset.

And, of course, the LOC is of vital importance to the development and progress of students in our schools. The more that students take on a growth mindset, the more they will take on board the LOC and be able to steer their own lives.

Thought control

This is once again to emphasise the idea that we do have control over our thoughts, particularly in terms of the challenges that we meet each and every day. We can take charge over the direction in which we want our thoughts to move. Hence, we can ask students to think about their thinking concerning things like whether something they are working on is impossible or simply a present challenge. The way they think about a challenge will significantly affect their approach and the ultimate outcome of anything that they do. Thought control is the first stage of the TEA-R model (see Chapter 7).

The FACT model is in many ways a summary and a reminder of a lot of the ideas that will be covered in this book. The more we are able to get students, and staff, to understand and use the thinking encompassed in the FACT model, the more we will be able to create a mindset for success in the school. It is something that we can apply to ourselves as educators and also use to help students. It is a model to support the social development of students, which in turn will help their learning development.

The level of mental health disorders found in young people today is at an all-time and very disturbing high. Some organisations report that one in ten children between the ages of 5 and 16 at any one time are experiencing psychological distress.[7] The findings of the National Institute of Mental Health in the United States are that 'Just over 20 percent (or 1 in 5) children, either currently or at some point during their life, have had a seriously debilitating mental disorder'.[8] Adopting a growth mindset will not ensure that a child never encounters something like depression, but Dweck's research shows that if an individual with a growth mindset enters a period of depression they will fight hard to get out of it by exploring different strategies and thinking processes.[9] On the other hand, people with a fixed mindset who become depressed will often dig themselves an ever bigger hole from which it becomes ever more difficult to escape. This is, therefore, another very powerful argument I present to head teachers as a justification for an ongoing programme of work on growth mindsets in order that it can become part of the culture in a school.

Developing resilience, perseverance, grit and well-being

I believe that one of the reasons why Dweck's idea of mindset has captured the imagination of so many educators and the general public is that it gets us back to understanding and focusing on the things that we believe to be essential elements of the experience that children should be having in our schools. There is a growing understanding that developing resilience, perseverance, grit and well-being in students are all things on which schools should be spending time and energy. There is overwhelming evidence that we can teach and enable children to develop these skills. For 11 years of my teaching life I had the privilege of working as a pastoral head dealing with the complex lives of thousands of young people between the ages of 11 and 18, while at the same time also teaching my own subject which was physics. There is no doubt which one of these (the pastoral work!) used up more of both my IQ and EQ energy. But I knew it was worthwhile. When students faced real challenges, perhaps from their home life, from relationships with peers

....

7   See, for example, http://www.youngminds.org.uk/training_services/policy/mental_health_statistics and https://www.mentalhealth.org.uk/a-to-z/c/children-and-young-people.

8   See http://www.nimh.nih.gov/health/statistics/prevalence/any-disorder-among-children.shtml.

9   Dweck, *Mindset*, p. 38.

or from the stress they were experiencing due to their academic studies, it was often impossible for them to focus on learning before they were able to overcome their other hurdles.

I have asked many parents what they most want from school for their children. I myself have three children, now all in their twenties, and like these parents I would have given the same response that I mostly hear from them. The things that parents say they want most for their child to experience and develop in school include happiness, confidence, friendship, kindness, a positive attitude, learning how to help others, being able to work in a team, learning how to stick at something and not give up, and many such similar things. At the same time, when I ask parents what they think schools provide and teach they will say things like academic learning, discipline, thinking skills, sports skills, maths, English, languages and the like.

Whether it is perception or reality, there is a clear disconnect between what many people believe schools are providing and what they want from schools. In brief, schools are involved in the business of accomplishment and preparing students for their movement into the adult world of work. This is very worthy and we are all in favour of students being encouraged to achieve great things in their school studies. This will bring a richness into their lives which will serve them well both now and in the future. It also opens up great opportunities and choices. However, it doesn't have to be all of one thing and none of the other. A school experience can be about both achievement and what we might call well-being. And, again, the research shows that the two things complement and support each other.

Higher levels of well-being produce better learning in our schools. For example it has been found that when children are in a good mood it supports their attention,[10] their creative thinking[11] and their holistic thinking.[12] Martin Seligman (the father of positive psychology) says that well-being should be taught

---

10 B. Fredrickson, What good are positive emotions? *Review of General Psychology*, 2(3) (1998), 300–319.

11 A. Isen, K. Daubman and G. Nowicki, Positive affect facilitates creative problem solving, *Journal of Personality and Social Psychology*, 52(6) (1987), 1122–1131.

12 A. Isen, A. Rosenzweig and M. Young, The influence of positive affect on clinical problem solving, *Medical Decision Making*, 11(3) (1991), 221–227.

in schools for three reasons: as an antidote to depression, to support greater life satisfaction and to help with learning and creative thinking.[13] Some parents, educators and politicians may argue that a focus on well-being will result in a lowering of student achievement. Some people in your own school community may also have this view. The research evidence, however, doesn't support this. Well-being improves students' engagement in learning and achievement, while at the same time supporting the development of skills that most people agree are of great importance.[14]

Many schools – your school perhaps – know that it is important to support children in this way. It is through a clear focus on well-being, as well as academic progress, that we provide the richest experience for the children which will then support them throughout their lives. Reminding ourselves of the disturbing evidence that 20% of young people will experience an episode of depression by the time they leave their secondary or high school,[15] it might be argued that well-being has to be an essential element of the taught curriculum in our schools. And this is where a mindset for success comes in.

The essential elements of well-being are resilience, perseverance and grit, and these are often referred to as if they are synonymous. It may be useful for us to make a distinction here between the three qualities.

- *Resilience* is the ability to recover after experiencing adversity or disappointment. The more resilience we have, the more we will be able to manage stressful situations. Dweck's research has shown that children with a growth mindset are able to bounce back from failure and treat it as a learning experience. It even appears to help individuals who suffer from some psychological stress.

----

13 See A. Tasman, J. Kay, J. A. Lieberman, M. B. First and M. Riba (eds), *Psychiatry*, 2 vols (4th rev. edn) (Chichester: Wiley-Blackwell, 2015), vol. 2, p. 493; and M. Seligman, R. Ernst, J. Gillham, K. Reivich and M. Linkins, Positive education: positive psychology and classroom interventions, *Oxford Review of Education*, 35(3) (2009), 293–311.

14 See Public Health England, *The Link Between Pupil Health and Wellbeing and Attainment: A Briefing for Head Teachers, Governors and Staff in Education Settings* (London: Public Health England, 2014).

15 P. Lewinsohn, P. Rohde, J. Seeley and S. Fischer, Age-cohort changes in the lifetime occurrence of depression and other mental disorders, *Journal of Abnormal Psychology*, 102(1) (1993), 110–120.

- *Perseverance* is linked with our determination to master a skill or complete a task – or, indeed, have a commitment to learning. Growth mindset children tend to see effort as the main contributing factor to their success. They therefore have a belief that a commitment to learning will bring just rewards and, equally, that skills can be developed if there is sufficient determination.

- *Grit* is our determination to strive for a long-term goal and in this way it is associated with self-control. Delaying short-term gratification necessitates a belief that a long-term goal can be achieved through the efforts we apply right now. The self-control that this requires will be better served by a growth mindset, which includes an understanding of how we can take control of our impulses by using both our brain and our mind in appropriate ways. (Angela Duckworth's TED talk on grit is worth watching.[16])

These are all attributes that are universally thought to be of great value to develop in our students. It seems to be without question that a school which works towards a mindset for success will support their students in each of these three ways.

Although it would seem likely that some people are more biologically predisposed to having greater resilience, perseverance and grit, the good news is that, like EQ and IQ, these traits can be developed. And a lot of this depends on the way people think, including their beliefs and attitudes which, in turn, can be positively influenced by developing a growth mindset.

---

16 A. Duckworth, Grit: the power of passion and perseverance [video], *TED.com* (April 2013). Available at: https://www.ted.com/talks/angela_lee_duckworth_grit_the_power_of_passion_and_ perseverance.

The ABCDE model and how to get out of a hole

One tool that I introduce to schools during the training I provide is the ABCDE model suggested by Martin Seligman in his book *Learned Optimism*.[17] A number of teachers have not only found this to be a useful tool to use with students but also to use themselves. Seligman has studied optimists and pessimists for over 30 years. Although he claims, like many other psychologists, that our level of optimism or pessimism is to some extent genetically influenced, at the same time he says that 'pessimism is escapable'. The ABCDE model (which stands for *adversity, belief, consequence, disputation* and *energisation*) is one way of enabling all of us to approach adversity in a more constructive way.

Whether you see yourself as an optimist or a pessimist, the ABCDE tool could prove to be useful. It is part of a set of cognitive skills that can support any of us to take more charge of our lives (where the LOC is more firmly established within us), resist the tendency to fall into depression and, as a result, help us to be more positive, feel better about ourselves and therefore be more able to move forward constructively in our lives.

The tremendous benefits for the students in using the ABCDE method is that they come to realise that they have a choice and some control over how they view a particular situation. They are then able to decide on new ways of experiencing the situation which can create positive patterns of thinking and remove or change negative ones. The most immediate benefit of the ABCDE method is realising you can choose how you think about a situation, which also means you can create new patterns of thinking, reinforce positive patterns and change negative ones.[18] It supports the TEA-R model that we will meet in Chapter 7. In brief, the TEA-R model describes how, if we control our thoughts, then this will impact upon our emotions, which then influences our actions, which ultimately brings about the results we get.

---

17 M. Seligman, *Learned Optimism: How to Change Your Mind and Your Life* (New York: Vintage Books, 2006).

18 See K. Reivich and A. Shatté, *The Resilience Factor: 7 Keys to Finding Your Inner Strength and Overcoming Life's Hurdles* (New York: Broadway Books, 2003).

The following is my adaptation of the ABCDE model (you can find a pro forma for this in Appendix C which you are free to photocopy and use with pupils or yourself). It is important that the person using this model writes down their thoughts and ideas.

1. Adversity

First of all we write down the adversity (misfortune, bad luck, trouble, difficulty) we are confronting. We also include the who, what, when and where of the situation. The more accurate and specific we can be the better, and we need to be as descriptive as possible (focusing on the facts) rather than bringing in our beliefs.

> Example from a member of staff: I didn't get the assistant head job in my school.
>
> Example from a pupil: I got another low mark in my maths test last week.

2. Belief

We now describe how we interpret the adversity. This is about our thoughts and not our feelings (our feelings are recorded in the consequence section below). If you say, 'I really think I'm hopeless,' then this is a belief, and if you say 'I'm never going to be able to do this,' this is also a belief.

> Example from a member of staff: This always happens to me – I knew they would pick John over me. It just goes to show that it's more about favouritism rather than what you can do and know.
>
> Example from a pupil: This proves once again that I just can't do maths.

3. Consequence

Here we record the consequences of our beliefs. This includes the feelings we have and the things we might have done (how we acted and behaved) as a result of those feelings. Again, we want to be very specific and record as many feelings and actions as possible. We also need to ask ourselves if the consequences do make sense based on our beliefs.

> Example from a member of staff: I feel really low. I just can't be bothered to put effort into preparing lessons the way I used to. And I find it hard to work with John now whereas before we were good friends. And I do think that my feelings and actions make sense based on my beliefs.

> Example from a pupil: I feel really thick. I have decided not to put any effort into my next maths test because what's the point? Of course what I am feeling and doing make complete sense based on my beliefs.

4. Disputation

We now try to find any evidence that brings into doubt our beliefs. We also try to think of other alternative beliefs about the adversity which are more positive and optimistic, or we might try to reframe our beliefs and put them into perspective in order to make them more accurate and optimistic. There are some useful phrases to use in the disputation stage to help us with our ideas:

a) Evidence: That's not completely true because …

b) Alternative: A more accurate way of seeing this is …

c) Putting it in perspective: The most likely outcome of this is … and I can … to handle it.

> Example from a member of staff:
> a) Evidence: That's not completely true because I had a promotion in the school just over 18 months ago.
> b) Alternative: A more accurate way of seeing this is that on this occasion John performed better in the interview.
> c) Putting it in perspective: The most likely outcome of this is that I still have a good job and I am respected in the school, and I can put a lot of my energy in my classroom into using the mindset strategies I have recently learned and this will help me to handle the immediate disappointment of not getting the job.

Example from a pupil:

a) Evidence: That's not completely true because I have had some good maths test results this year.

b) Alternative: A more accurate way of seeing this is that it demonstrates that there are some things I need to ask my teacher about so next time I will have a better chance of doing well in the test.

c) Putting it in perspective: The most likely outcome of this is that I can find other ways of studying, and I can enjoy going to the cinema with my friends so that it will lift my spirits and help me to handle the present disappointment.

5. Energisation

Energisation is what we feel and get from redirecting our thoughts and attention. We can write down here how the disputation has enabled us to change the energy level we feel, our mood and how we behave. We also might add here any solutions that we now see that we were unable to see before.

Example from a member of staff: I feel a lot more positive. I have some ideas that I would like to share with John that can help him and would interest me as well. I really do get a lot of enjoyment from teaching and this present situation is not going to make this change. I think I will ask the head teacher to give me some feedback on the interview and ask for her views about what I might do next.

Example from a pupil: I feel a lot less down. I know my level in maths is not great at the moment, but I have taken on board the things that I have learned in school about mindsets and I am determined that I am going to do the best that I can. There is no point in me comparing myself with other students in the class. I want to just focus on what I can do to improve.

This first part of this book has looked at why changing mindsets in our schools is of the utmost importance. Developing growth mindsets in both adults and students will have a positive impact on both the academic and personal development of our students, and, as we have seen, these two dimensions have a symbiotic relationship that also creates great synergy. In particular, the development of what we might call the 'soft skills' of students very much supports their academic progress. But what exactly do we mean by mindsets? And more specifically, what does

Carol Dweck mean when she refers to growth and fixed mindsets? This is what we will focus our attention on in Part II.

On our journey we will visit our mind and our brain to examine the key things that support the development of a growth mindset. We will see how our mind has two parts, the conscious and subconscious, and how we can use affirmations to help us achieve what we want in our lives. We will exercise ourselves by climbing the competency ladder and come to realise that practice on its own does not lead to increased mastery, but that deliberate practice is the key to significant progress. In developing a mindset for success in a school we will also see how coaching supports the empowerment of all individuals, both adults and children, as they strive for greater happiness, fulfilment and success. Hattie's research of the research (or meta-research) will be referred to as evidence of how Dweck's findings are echoed in other studies around the world. And we will reflect on how it is the small things that we often do in schools, and indeed in our lives, that lead on to significant and long lasting change. Finally, you will be invited to participate in a game show called *Let's Make a Deal* where you have the chance of winning the star prize of a brand new car – or a goat! So let's see how you get on …

Part II

What mindsets are all about

Chapter 2
What do we mean by mindsets?

What is fixed?

A fundamental part of Carol Dweck's work on mindsets concerns the beliefs we have about whether intelligence and talent are fixed or malleable. And the interesting thing is that no matter what the 'truth' is about this, it is what we believe that will influence how we learn both in school and for the rest of our lives. It is our beliefs about intelligence and talent that significantly determine our approach to learning, challenges and being able to bounce back from adversity. As most of what we do takes place subconsciously, it is our deep-seated beliefs that drive our actions. And, therefore, it is these beliefs that we need to reflect upon in order to make a conscious decision to change them, if we decide that this is appropriate.

Let us now look at the evidence about both talent and intelligence (or IQ). The first thing that needs to be said is that the research indicates clearly that talent is not the dominant factor that drives and determines success. One piece of research, for example, concludes that 'The evidence we have surveyed ... does not support the talent account, according to which excelling is a consequence of possessing innate gifts.'[1] Instead, it is found that success in any complex task is primarily determined by effort, so as teachers we need to make this very clear to all the students we teach. If you were to ask a 4-year-old child if she could play a violin the answer you might get is likely to be 'Not yet'. A year or two later the answer to the same question might well change to 'No, I can't'. The child has changed from having what Dweck refers to as a growth mindset to a fixed mindset, and their belief affects not only the present but also the future.

....

1   M. Howe, J. Davidson and J. Sloboda, Innate talents: reality or myth? *Behavioral and Brain Sciences*, 21(3) (1998), 399–442 at 407.

We sometimes find ourselves making assertions like, 'I can't do maths,' 'I can't spell' or 'I'm hopeless at sport'. None of these things might matter a lot to us. We may not be bothered if we believe that, for example, we can't draw a face particularly well. But what we are doing is expressing a fixed mindset view of how we believe we *are*. The danger comes when we hold similar beliefs about things that we would really like to change, because these beliefs may be impacting on our prospects of future success. Even more importantly, the beliefs teachers have about students will be picked up by them even if we do not verbalise them. (This links with the Pygmalion effect and 'thin slice' that were discussed in the introduction.)

The old debate about whether it is nature or nurture, genes or the environment, that governs our success in life is no longer the issue. There is a rich interaction between the two. As Dweck says, 'genes require input from the environment to work properly'.[2] We all start, therefore, with our unique genetic code which influences our initial temperaments and attitudes. However, experience, training, learning and, what we will call here and throughout this book, *deliberate practice*, all play a significant part in our development and progress through life. Robert Sternberg, professor of psychology at Oklahoma State University, says that achieving expertise is not down to 'some fixed prior ability, but purposeful engagement'.[3] The French psychologist Alfred Binet, inventor of the IQ test, believed that it was not always those who started out the smartest who ended up the smartest:

> A few modern philosophers assert that an individual's intelligence is a fixed quantity, a quantity which cannot be increased. We must protest and react against this brutal pessimism ... With practice, training, and above all, method, we manage to increase our attention, our memory, our judgment and literally to become more intelligent than we were before.[4]

When the French government passed laws in the early 1990s which meant that all children had to attend school, Binet was asked to come up with a way to identify those students who may need special help with their studies. He developed a psychometric test in order to single out those students whose mental age did not match their chronological age, based on a series of averages. The test was never

---

2   Dweck, *Mindset*, p. 2.

3   Quoted in A. Elliot and C. Dweck, *Handbook of Competence and Motivation* (New York: Guilford Press, 2005), p. 5.

4   A. Binet, Les idées modernes sur les enfants, *Population*, 29(3) (1974), 664 (orig. pub. 1909).

intended to be a measure of fixed intelligence, and yet today IQ is often talked about by the general public, as well as in schools, in a way that implies that it is innate. Even if we claim to believe that IQ is not fixed, teachers may still inadvertently give out messages that tell a very different story.

As teachers we need to spread the message that what we achieve in life is not established at birth or at any other point in our lives. We have the constant potential to develop and grow. Any measure that is taken of us, by ourselves or others, is merely a snapshot recording current reality at a moment in time. Once we understand and accept that our mindset plays a profound part in how we lead our lives and the things that we achieve in life, then the rest is down to us. We can flick the switch and accept responsibility for who we are, what we do, how we do it and the results we get. Or we can remain on the effect side of life, always believing that we are what we are and that this, together with circumstances beyond our control, shapes our destiny. All of this is about where we consider the LOC to be. Does it rest inside of us so that we take on responsibility for our life, or does it exist external to us so that we are merely blown by the winds of circumstance? The importance of our decision is immense. The impact for us as teachers is also profound. The imperative for us to develop an understanding in students that for each of us success comes from taking real ownership for our own personal development, and the fact that this can be achieved by adopting a growth mindset, needs to become our top priority.

Dweck makes a distinction between the two extreme types of mindset. In reality, none of us will sit at either extreme in all aspects of our lives. However, the more we can encourage students to adopt a growth mindset, the more they will feel in control of their own learning and their lives in general.

Fixed mindset people believe:

- Personal qualities (including intelligence) are impossible to change.

- They need to prove themselves over and over.

- Overall, intelligence is static (this leads to a desire to look smart and a tendency to avoid challenges).

- That when things are challenging they might as well give up.

- Effort is a waste of time.

- Negative feedback should be ignored.

- The success of others is a threat to them.

Growth mindset people believe:

- Their basic qualities can be cultivated through their effort.

- They can change and grow through effort, application and experience.

- Their overall intelligence is something that can be developed, which leads to embracing challenges.

- Challenge is a source for learning, effort is vital, and resilience and persistence in the face of setbacks are important.

- Effort is the path to mastery.

- There is a lot to learn from criticism.

- Lessons and inspiration can be found in the success of others.

Dweck's findings about the various differences between people with fixed and growth mindsets are often startling and have enormous consequences for our work as educators. For example, her studies clearly show that those with growth mindsets (compared with those with fixed mindsets) are far more accurate at estimating both their performance and present ability, far more open to information about their current abilities, even if it is unflattering, and far more able to identify their own strengths and weaknesses. The clear and optimistic message of Dweck's research is that we can change our mindset. Mindsets are about beliefs and beliefs can be changed – if we want to change them.

Other contrasting beliefs of those with fixed and growth mindsets that are important for us to be aware of include:

- **Prove or learn.** Those with a fixed mindset want to prove they are smart or talented. Those with a growth mindset want to stretch themselves – to learn something new.

- **Failure.** For those with a fixed mindset, failure is about having setbacks. Losing a job, failing in a game or being rejected in romance all indicate to the fixed mindset person that they are not smart, talented or gifted. For those with a growth mindset, real failure would occur only if they don't try and as a result they don't grow. (Even if those with a growth mindset have failures along the way these are simply viewed as learning experiences.)

- **Trying.** For those with a fixed mindset, trying is a bad thing. It indicates that they are not smart, talented or gifted: if they were smart/talented/gifted they would not have to put in effort. For those with a growth mindset, trying is a natural thing to do because, with time and deliberate practice, it makes them smarter or more talented.

It has also been found that those with a fixed mindset tend to take the safe option. They don't want to take on challenges in case they fail, because failure would indicate that they are not intelligent. In *Mindset*, Dweck refers to studies that were done looking at the brainwaves of people at a lab in Columbia where it was found that those with a fixed mindset were only interested in information about whether the answers they had given to hard questions were right or wrong. Their brainwave patterns showed that they weren't interested in information that could help them to learn. On the other hand, the growth mindset people showed interest in finding out how they could improve their knowledge and finding out how they could learn more effectively.

The diagrams below summarise some of the key beliefs of those people with a growth mindset and those with a fixed mindset. You will know students in your own school who predominantly possess the kinds of beliefs shown here for fixed mindset individuals. One important thing for us to be aware of from the outset is not to label individuals in our schools as having fixed or growth mindsets. Rather, we can refer to the thought processes or beliefs that we all have and which can influence us to behave as if we have a growth mindset or a fixed mindset. And, of course, our thoughts and beliefs can change, therefore encouraging us to behave more like a growth or fixed mindset person. So, if an individual is displaying fixed mindset behaviours as an outcome of their fixed mindset thoughts, then we must view this as a temporary situation or condition which can be changed if the individual decides to take action. Labelling a student as having a fixed mindset may give them the impression that we believe that this is something which is permanent, when we know that this is definitely not the case.

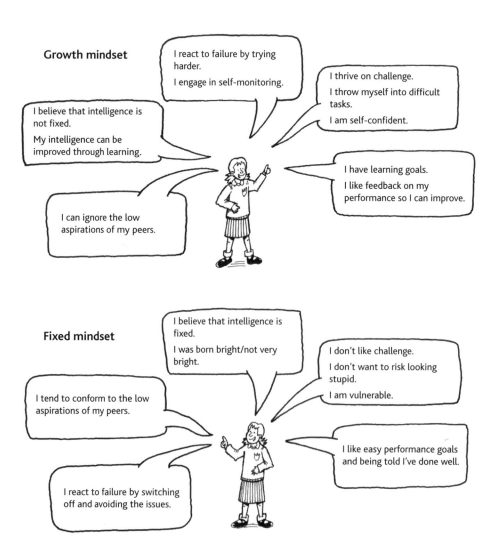

Growth mindset

I react to failure by trying harder.
I engage in self-monitoring.

I thrive on challenge.
I throw myself into difficult tasks.
I am self-confident.

I believe that intelligence is not fixed.
My intelligence can be improved through learning.

I have learning goals.
I like feedback on my performance so I can improve.

I can ignore the low aspirations of my peers.

Fixed mindset

I believe that intelligence is fixed.
I was born bright/not very bright.

I don't like challenge.
I don't want to risk looking stupid.
I am vulnerable.

I tend to conform to the low aspirations of my peers.

I like easy performance goals and being told I've done well.

I react to failure by switching off and avoiding the issues.

None of us have any idea to what level any individual might personally develop through effort and time. And yet the school process seems to categorise students in such a way that they are often pushed towards a fixed mindset. I am not suggesting that there is a deliberate attempt to do this. But with the knowledge that we now have about how the brain works, how people operate and how to get the very best from them, it is no longer possible for any of us in education to persist with a system that simply does not work as well as it could.

All of us, as educators, have a part to play in changing the system. If we can gather a group of like-minded people around us then the impact will be even more powerful. As the well-known saying counsels, 'Never doubt that a small group of thoughtful, committed citizens can change the world; indeed, it's the only thing that ever has.' Failure must be encouraged, as ridiculous as this will seem at first. Of course I am not saying that we encourage students to fail. We want them to succeed. But high levels of success will only come from a process where effort is valued above all. Failure is an essential part of a system that develops a growth mindset in all those involved, whether that system is a family, school or business.

Moving from a fixed to a growth mindset involves a shift in how we think and speak about ourselves and others. It is about defining our actions rather than our being. Teachers know that it is more effective in situations where a student has behaved inappropriately to blame the behaviour and not the individual. If a student swears, for example, it is easy to see the different impact that the following two comments made by a teacher can have.

a)   You are a foul-mouthed person.

b)   That kind of language is not acceptable in this school.

In (a) we have labelled the individual. We have, in effect, made our own fixed mindset evaluation of them that, if accepted by them, could persuade them to have a similarly fixed mindset. The consequences of this would be significant in many ways. For example, in similar situations in the future they are likely to use inappropriate language because they have accepted that they are a 'foul-mouthed person' and so must act in this way. They will think, 'How can I change when *I am* this way?'

In (b) we have referred to the behaviour. Behaviour is something that it is possible to change, if there is a desire to do so. If we had added to this statement 'and I don't expect this from you', then we are reinforcing the message that swearing is not something that we see as being part of their personality.

I am suggesting that, in a similar way to when we talk about behaviour, we, as teachers, must adopt a way of talking to students that removes any reference to their talent, giftedness or innate intelligence. We replace these references with comments about their desire to learn, commitment to working to achieve success, positive approach in the face of a challenge, willingness to try things that seem difficult and love of learning from mistakes they make. This will serve them well not only in their ability to succeed in school but also in their future life.

> Did you know that ... NASA has rejected people who had simply had a track record of success in favour of those who had had significant failures and bounced back from them?
>
> Carol Dweck[5]

Another consequence Dweck discovered of those people who have a fixed mindset was that they tend to shirk responsibility, cheat, lie and even blame others. She found that when 12- and 13-year-old students were asked about how they might respond in the future to a poor test result they had just received in a new course, those with fixed and growth mindsets gave very different answers. Those with a growth mindset said they would study harder for the next test. Incredible as it may seem, those with a fixed mindset said they would study less hard. The logic of the fixed mindset students was that if they were no good at the subject (as demonstrated by their test result), then what was the point of trying? In addition, they were prepared to consider cheating because this would offer them a way to succeed that would hide their lack of ability.

To recover their self-esteem, fixed mindset students tend to look for people who have done worse than themselves. This occurred with a group of college students who after a test were given the opportunity to acquire further learning by studying

....

5   Dweck, *Mindset*, p. 29.

the papers of other students. You can probably guess what happened here. Those with a growth mindset welcomed the opportunity to look at the test papers of students who had done very well so that they could learn and correct any mistakes they may have made. Those with a fixed mindset chose to look at the test papers of those students who had done worse than them so that they could feel better about themselves and repair their self-esteem. I suspect that these kinds of findings are ringing bells in your head as, indeed, they did with me; you will probably know of many students who display similar behaviour patterns. In the past you may have felt despair and wondered how (or if it was possible) to do something about this. Now you know that you can. Once again, mindsets can be changed. They are simply beliefs, and for any belief the switch can be flicked to offer the opposite belief. The key is for us to provide the evidence for students that drives the emotional desire to change their belief.

Mindsets and depression

The importance of Dweck's research also spreads to how we might deal with depression in society. It is amazing to us now to think that up until about 40 years ago, many in the field of psychology believed that children were incapable of experiencing depression. Research now reveals 'that children with mood disorders like depression are more than five times more likely to attempt suicide than children not affected by such problems.'[6]

In the United States, the National Institute of Mental Health estimates that at least 2.5% of children under the age of 18 (1.8 million children) are 'severely depressed'.[7] The American Academy of Child and Adolescent Psychiatry places the number at 5% (3.6 million).[8] A number of authorities believe that depression remains severely under-diagnosed and that an incredible and disturbing one in four children will experience a severe episode of depression by their 18th birth-

···

6   D. Fassler and L. Dumas, *Help Me, I'm Sad* (New York: Viking, 1997).

7   See http://www.nimh.nih.gov/health/statistics/prevalence/any-disorder-among-children.shtml.

8   See http://www.aacap.org/aacap/Families_and_Youth/Resource_Centers/Depression_Resource_Center/Home.aspx.

day.[9] It is clear that depression can be a dangerous illness. Teachers know from their own experience of dealing with children that those who are under stress, experience loss, have attentional disorders like attention deficit hyperactivity disorder (ADHD), have learning challenges, have behavioural issues or suffer from anxiety disorders are at a higher risk from depression.

In addition, the evidence shows that depression tends to run in families.[10] Depression impacts on the academic success of young people, which in turn can generate a downward cycle. At home they can be difficult to deal with, even if the family is trying to understand and support them. Trying to understand what someone is going through when they are depressed can be difficult; total empathy may be an impossibility. To add to this, the depressed individual's judgement deteriorates, interests wane and failure occurs. The emotional costs for an individual, a family and at a societal level is vast, and the suggestion is that this is a growing problem. Teachers who develop an understanding of mindsets, and how they can apply the ideas in their classrooms, will be in a strong position to support individuals suffering from or in danger of sinking into depression. A significant way of doing this can be through providing young people with a clear understanding of how they can adopt a personally supportive growth mindset.

This is not to suggest that adopting a growth mindset will necessarily stop an individual from becoming depressed. Dweck found that students at her university with both a fixed and a growth mindset could at times suffer from depression. Although those with a fixed mindset tended to show more depression, there were plenty of students with a growth mindset who suffered too. The difference occurred in the way that the two groups dealt with it. Those with a fixed mindset tended to go through a negative TEA-R cycle (negative thoughts, emotions and actions bring about our results, as described in Chapter 7) as they stewed on their situation. They were inclined to dig ever bigger holes for themselves and labelled themselves as being unworthy and incompetent. As a result, they tended to stop studying and failed to hand in assignments on time.

....

9   Fassler and Dumas, *Help Me, I'm Sad.*

10   *National Institutes of Health* (2013). Common Genetic Factors Found in 5 Mental Disorders. Available at: https://www.nih.gov/news-events/nih-research-matters/common-genetic-factors-found-5-mental-disorders.

On the other hand, Dweck found something amazing with those with a growth mindset. They tended to fight hard to get out of the depressed state. This helped them to get on with their lives and to do their schoolwork. It truly seemed to be the case that their determination increased even more when they felt really bad. Initially when I have told people about this during mindset training some have suggested that it might just be that the different students had different temperaments or natures. However, Dweck is very firm in saying that 'Temperament certainly plays a role but mindset is the most important part of the story.'[11] In addition, this is supported by the fact that when students were taught about growth mindsets they were able to significantly change the way they dealt with a depressed mood. The research suggests that supporting students to adopt a growth mindset will help them cope with the challenges of life in an effective way. It is therefore important to teach students about growth mindsets because it will not just affect their academic performance but also broader, and perhaps even more important, aspects of their lives.

As Malcolm Gladwell has suggested, we need to create a society that moves away from a culture of praising and putting on a pedestal those people who seem to achieve great success with ease.[12] They become like heroes for the perceived inborn ability they possess when, in fact, most great achievers will put their personal success down to hard work. The problem with perpetuating the adoration of talent is that it fosters a fixed mindset approach. Many people who have a fixed mindset like the idea that talent is the dominant factor influencing an individual's success because it removes from them the need to put in effort, which they regard as an indicator that a person is lacking in some way. It enables them to remove the LOC from within themselves so they can comfortably sit back in a restrictive comfort zone, repeating the well-known chant of 'It's not my fault'. Taking talent out of the equation, however, robs those with a fixed mindset of excuses. They now have to accept that effort is the key determinant of success. In addition, putting effort into something requires people to move outside their comfort zone. Those with a fixed mindset will find this the hardest to do because they will be exposing themselves to potential failure. A shift to a growth mindset involves people moving from the 'effect' side of life to the 'cause' side. It is easy to blame external events and life's

---

11 Dweck, *Mindset*, p. 39.

12 M. Gladwell, *Outliers: The Story of Success* (New York: Little, Brown and Co., 2008).

circumstances for our lack of success. When we do this we are sitting on the effect side of life. When we take full responsibility for our outcomes and accept that we can grow and develop, if we are determined to do so, then we move to the cause side of life.

Dweck's research confirms what we all know – that children are born with a desire to find out, to learn and to develop. They have a growth mindset. Somewhere along their journey in life many adopt a fixed mindset. This cannot be allowed to continue and we, as teachers, have a considerable role to play in influencing this and therefore having a lasting impact on so many of the lives of the young people we teach.

Transition time

Let us now return to a topic that was mentioned at the beginning of Chapter 1. Moving from a primary school to a secondary school in the UK (or elementary school to junior high in the United States) can be a difficult time for many students. You may recall the sense of apprehension that you yourself felt during this time. Dweck studied how students performed throughout this transition, and in particular she looked at how their maths grades altered over the next two years. Well, you may have guessed, but what Dweck found was that the grades of those students with a fixed mindset declined over the next two years whereas those who had a growth mindset showed an increase in their grades.[13]

If their maths grades could be used to determine their level of IQ (at the very least their maths IQ), then clearly something very odd is going on here. The results of this experiment provide evidence that IQ is not fixed. Furthermore, it shows how what kind of mindset a student has, either fixed or growth, will strongly influence their learning and academic performance.

....

13 See L. S. Blackwell, K. H. Trzesniewski and C. S. Dweck, Implicit theories of intelligence predict achievement across an adolescent transition: a longitudinal study and an intervention, *Child Development*, 78(1) (2007), 246–263 at 251.

On transition to junior high school, the maths grades of fixed mindset students declined and continued to decline over the next 2 years.

On transition to junior high school, the maths grades of growth mindset students increased.

The self-talk going on in our heads concerning whether we believe our intelligence can grow has a significant impact on the way our intelligence does grow. Adopting the fixed mindset collection of beliefs may not only restrict our intellectual growth but actually cause it to decline over time. We might conclude that, in a paradoxical way, a belief that intelligence is fixed can produce evidence that contradicts this belief by actually causing our intelligence to reduce!

Damned data

The ignorance of youth, or lack of knowing 'the truth' as determined by 'experts' in a given field, can sometimes act as an asset in terms of students' learning. The great American pianist, Ruth Laredo, looking back on how she tackled the challenges posed by Ravel said: 'I learned the Ravel repertoire mostly when I was so young that the extreme difficulties somehow didn't bother me. *Gaspard de la nuit* came into my life at fifteen. I just didn't know how hard it was.'[14] There is a very real learning health warning here about the negative impact that can come from the massive amount of data that schools now have on student progress, and the self-fulfilling nature of this both in terms of the pupils themselves and the

....

14 Quoted in E. B. Brooks, Tales of statisticians: George B Dantzig, *Umass.edu* (2001). Available at: https://www.umass.edu/wsp/resources/tales/dantzig.html.

teachers that teach them. If teachers didn't make assumptions about how difficult work was going to be for some students, and the students themselves didn't make these assumptions either, then who knows what they may be able to achieve.

Whether we believe in prodigies or not, the wonderful news is that within each individual there lies a great wealth of potential waiting to be nourished, developed and released. As educators, we need to ask ourselves, 'How can I get the best from this student?' and not, 'Do they have ability?' I firmly believe that if we use the information in this book then we may see magic happen before our eyes. Students will astound all of us with what they are able to accomplish.

Benjamin Bloom, famous for the creation of his taxonomy, concluded after 40 years of research concerning learning that 'What any person in the world can learn, *almost* all persons can learn, *if* provided with the appropriate prior and current conditions of learning.'[15] It seems to be that there are 2–3% of pupils who have severe impairments and at the other end of the spectrum 1–2% who are born with apparently heightened abilities, but the rest of students are like you and me – possessing a wealth of potential that is waiting to be harvested.

Teacher beliefs and student success

Now let us return to the impact that our beliefs as teachers have on the students we teach. Some teachers might think that what they believe about students in general, as well as individual students, has little to do with their learning. 'After all,' they may claim, 'it is up to the students how they respond to the learning opportunity that I present to them.' What they are missing out on here is the clear part that they play in the learning process, and this is not just about simply providing the students with the information, instructions and structure of the lessons. Machines could do that, and indeed computers do. What matters is the relationship between the students and the teacher, and a key part of that involves the overt and covert messages that the teacher communicates

....

15 B. Bloom and L. Sosniak, *Developing Talent in Young People* (New York: Ballantine Books, 1985), p. 7.

to the students. A teacher's beliefs play a key part in how successful they are as a teacher.

Many of us know this, either instinctively or through investigation, experience and learning. However, some teachers with fixed mindsets will say that they *know* at the beginning of an academic year how well certain students will do. They have studied past performance, examination results and predicted grades and as a result adopt a Newtonian approach to education. (Those of you who remember Sir Isaac Newton from your science lessons may also recall that Newton described a deterministic world where future outcomes could be predicted with precision from past events, like billiard balls colliding on a table.) In a similar way, these teachers believe they can predict the outcome of students from the pattern that has so far been formed, with little chance of students changing direction.

I have had the opportunity and immense privilege of working with teachers and leaders in around 15 countries. When I ask them about the kinds of qualities and actions of a great mentor, coach or leader in their lives, they always place 'they believed in me' near or at the top of the list. In an effective (or ineffective) way, every teacher is a mentor, coach and leader in the classroom and their deepest beliefs play a fundamental role in their success and the resultant learning of the students. The beliefs of a teacher filter through to the students and create a feedback loop that inevitably leads to a self-fulfilling prophecy.

The impact of the mindset of teachers on the learning of students is exemplified by a study carried out by Falko Rheinberg, a researcher from Germany.[16] The results are startlingly clear. You see, those teachers with a fixed mindset knew how well students would do. They knew how intelligent students were. They could predict how students would do. And they did this very well every time! The students who had previously performed well continued to do so. Those who had previously performed poorly continued to do so. In the world view of these fixed mindset teachers it was as if the Newtonian billiard balls, representing the past performance of students, clearly predicted their future outcomes. Maybe they could be given a little more of a push. Sometimes they could be slowed down. But

16 F. Rheinberg, R. Vollmeyer and W. Rollett, Motivation and action in self-regulated learning. In M. Boekaerts, P. Pintrich and M. Zeidner (eds), *Handbook of Self-Regulation: Theory, Research and Application* (San Diego, CA: Academic Press, 2005), pp. 503–509.

essentially, for these teachers, the past largely defined the future. In other words intelligence was fixed. But something quite different occurred with the students in the classes of teachers with growth mindsets. These students were the fortunate ones because all of them advanced. Their teachers preached and practised a growth mindset and the students benefited from this. In fact, the differences in how groups of students had previously performed remarkably disappeared.

Students need to know that we have confidence in them. Outstanding teachers believe in their students. And this is something that has to be real and not fake. Students instantly know if their teacher is faking it. They will pick up on the 'thin slice' that runs through a teacher like the message that runs through a stick of rock. The interesting thing is that, once again, mindsets can be altered in teachers just as much as in students. It may require a little work and it does require a change of one or more beliefs, but with desire it is possible to acquire a growth mindset. And once we have a growth mindset we will find evidence everywhere to confirm that we are correct in our beliefs. This is the way our minds work. We want to find that the external world matches our internal description of it. The RAS will once again ensure that this happens. This is why teachers who believe that 'students are impolite these days' will find examples of this all around them. On the other hand, teachers who believe that students have good intentions will equally be on the lookout for this and, through their subconscious mind and their RAS, find numerous examples to prove their belief every day. And you can probably imagine the feedback loop set up here between the teacher and the student. Without any words necessarily being spoken they both *know* what the truth is!

Having now established that working to support students to have a growth mindset is of immense importance in terms of their academic and personal development, and with the clarity we now have concerning what mindsets are all about, in the next chapter we will look at how we can further support the growth of all the students we teach.

Chapter 3
Trying to get better

Practice doesn't make perfect

To become outstanding at anything requires time and effort. We either accept this and put in the required work to ensure success, or we might decide to take on a different, more defeatist attitude that will not support our movement forward – more akin to Kurt Cobain's professed comment that 'Practice makes perfect, but nobody's perfect, so why practice?'

Getting better at anything requires deliberate practice. But what exactly is this? Well, the first thing to say is that in order for us to get better at something, develop a new skill or increase our expertise, it is essential that we commit ourselves to practice and more practice. However, the type of practice that we do will significantly impact on the way that we make progress. So, we can say that the quality of the practice, as well as the quantity of the practice, is what makes the difference. In their seminal paper, 'The role of deliberate practice in the acquisition of expert performance', K. Anders Ericsson and his colleagues set out the case for deliberate practice, including the proposition that expert level performance is primarily determined by the type and quantity of practice rather than some innate, inborn talent.[1] In my seminars, I ask the audience the question, 'How many of you are better at driving a car today than you were 12 months ago?' Most people say that they are no better, and some even say that they think they are a worse driver today than they were 12 months or a few years ago. And yet, they have all been *practising* their driving, in the sense of driving maybe every day, without getting any better. This is an example of how repetition of an activity, on its own, will not necessarily lead to higher levels of performance.

....

1   K. A. Ericsson, R. Krampe and C. Tesch-Romer, The role of deliberate practice in the acquisition of expert performance, *Psychological Review*, 100(3) (1993), 363–406.

There have been just a few people, out of many hundreds, who have said that they believe their driving is better now than it was 12 months ago. When I ask them why this is, in one case a teacher told me that she had only passed her driving test in the last 18 months and felt that she was still improving her driving, including parking and driving on motorways. In another case, a teacher told me that a few months ago he had taken a National Speed Awareness Course as an alternative to having fixed penalty points on his licence and a fine. He said that the course was 'a real eye-opener' and had made him think carefully about his driving and how he could improve it. Both of these examples illustrate how it takes a special kind of practice to enable us to increase our expertise. The recently qualified driver was constantly thinking about how she could improve her driving skills, and the driver who had committed a speeding offence was now, once again, reflecting on his personal driving and how this might be improved and made safer for himself and everyone else.

From his research into what makes some people excel in a given activity, Ericsson concluded that 'we argue that the differences between expert performers and normal adults reflect a life-long period of deliberate effort to improve performance in a specific domain.'[2] In other words, experts are constantly striving to improve what they do. It is more about their perseverance, resilience and grit than any inborn talent. Deliberate practice is a highly structured activity that is focused on continual improvement. In the classroom, the student needs to know where they are now in their learning, where they want to get to and the next deliberate practice steps they need to take to begin to bridge the gap. Deliberate practice can be fun, but not always, and generally it requires a significant amount of determination. Ericsson concludes that optimal learning and improved performance require four essential deliberate practice components:

1. Motivation and effort. For a student to improve on what they presently do they must be motivated to carry out the deliberate practice and be willing to commit themselves to putting in the effort that is required.

2. Pre-existing knowledge should be taken into account. The design of the task given by the teacher to a student should be based on what the student

....

2   Ericsson et al., The role of deliberate practice, 400.

already knows, and described with a clarity that enables the student to rapidly understand what they are required to do.

3. Immediate informative feedback. The student will be able to make swift progress if they are provided with immediate feedback that allows them to understand how they are performing and progressing on the task.

4. Repetition. The student should be given the opportunity to carry out the same or similar tasks in order to reinforce their learning and to try to improve on the task each time.

Deliberate practice is about continual challenge, understanding any present weaknesses and working on how to improve on these areas. It takes time, lots of time, which is part of an investment in long-term progress and success. In fact, according to Ericsson, it will take 10,000 hours of deliberate practice to become an expert in almost anything.[3] If you work this out, you will find that it would take you 10 years of practising for 20 hours per week and for 50 weeks each year to have completed those 10,000 hours.

Deliberate practice is transformative and this is what we require in schools both in terms of student learning and teacher development. But is transformative practice taking place in our schools and classrooms already? Well, the answer is both yes and no. Research gives a very mixed picture. Some things that certain teachers do in their classrooms are truly inspirational and result in transformation. But we have to accept that in some classrooms teachers do not enable the students to make the kind of progress of which they are capable. Professor John Hattie's research indicates that some students achieve no more from being in lessons than they would if they did not attend these lessons.[4]

The potential that lies within all of us to achieve extraordinary things is a theme that runs throughout this book. I am not arguing that with the correct application anyone could become a Rosalind Franklin, Albert Einstein or Richard Wagner. But what I am saying is that modern day research makes it clear that the true potential which lies within each of us is probably always going to remain a mystery

....

3   Ericsson et al., The role of deliberate practice, 393–394.

4   J. Hattie, *Visible Learning for Teachers* (London: Routledge, 2012).

and unknown. However, we can say, with integrity, to all of our students, 'If you apply yourself with passion, dedication, deliberate practice, toil and persistence there is no way of knowing what you might achieve.'

But the truth is that the easy way out is not to think and not to put in the effort required for us to improve. Sitting back in the cosy armchair comfort zone may appear to be a more attractive option. We meet students, and indeed other adults, who take this path of least resistance. And there can be a temptation for teachers to do the same, relying on old tried and tested, but maybe ineffective, methods that require little imagination because, as the old saying goes, 'Thinking is the hardest work there is, which is the probable reason why so few engage in it.' But if we do make the effort, then we will begin on the journey of climbing the ladder of competence.

Climbing the competency ladder

Once the children understand that practice itself does not get them to a higher level of learning, then we can introduce to them another model which illustrates how we all go through a series of steps – or up a ladder – of learning which takes us progressively to a higher level of understanding. The competency ladder model takes us through at least five steps, as follows.

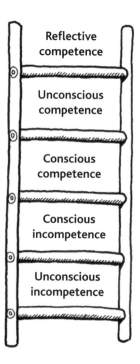

Unconscious incompetence

At the lowest level of unconscious incompetence we lack knowledge, skill and ability in a particular area but we are not aware of this. We have a blind spot. We may ask a child in a classroom what it is that they don't understand about a particular topic and they reply 'I don't know'. They simply can't articulate what it is that they don't know because at this time the whole topic seems so obscure. An example of this that most of us will have experienced is when we begin to learn to drive a car. We may have all sat in a car before we took the decision to learn how to drive, but once we are behind the wheel we may suddenly realise that we don't really understand how to get the car moving.

Conscious incompetence

At the next level of conscious incompetence we understand and realise the aspects that we must work on in order to get better at the skill we want to learn. And in order to get better, we realise that we have to try to do things that we may find difficult, and in the process we will make many mistakes. In terms of developing a growth mindset, it is essential that we emphasise to children the importance of this step. This is all part of great learning. If we are determined and display grit, resilience and perseverance (the things we describe here as being key aspects of developing a growth mindset), then we will progress from this stage. Using the example of driving a car, we may now realise that a hill start is complex, and in the process of practising this we may stall the car many times and get frustrated.

Conscious competence

At the level of conscious competence we know how to do something, but in order to do it well we need to use a lot of deliberate effort. In the car example, at this stage we may have just passed our driving test, but driving a car is still something that requires a lot of conscious attention. We may be able to park the car but it takes a lot of focused concentration.

Unconscious competence

By the level of unconscious competence the learning or skill has become second nature. We can perform the activity with relative ease, with much of it being done by our unconscious (or subconscious) mind. This is where, in terms of driving a car, we may arrive at our workplace – somewhere we have been to many times before – with a sense of amazement that we have done this without easily remembering the journey. In general, we don't need to be overly concerned about this because our RAS should be alerting our conscious mind to unexpected and unusual incidents as we drive along. This level can be sometimes regarded as the highest and most desirable state that we can reach. However, there are distinct dangers associated with unconscious competence. For example, we are no longer performing deliberate practice, and therefore a skill that we presently have may plateau and not get any better. In fact, we may find that we become less accomplished in this area as time goes by. Complacency can set in.

As with all professions, this can happen in teaching unless we are constantly looking to improve on the skills we have. A teacher may, for example, have taught in the same way for 20 years and find that their classroom techniques are no longer as successful as they were a number of years ago. Without being conscious of exactly what they do and why they do it, they will find it hard to adjust their practice. They may then externalise what is happening to them and blame factors that are beyond their apparent control, such as a change in society, different demands by parents or a lack of respect from pupils. In other words, they push the LOC away from themselves.

Another danger associated with unconscious competence is that because we now carry out the task without a great deal of conscious thought, it is often difficult for us to explain to another person how we achieve the task with apparent ease. In terms of sharing good practice with colleagues in schools, it is essential that we can articulate to each other the steps required to achieve higher levels of competence.

Reflective competence

Reflective competence is the level where we are able to operate for some of the time at an unconsciously competent level but at the same time reflect on what we need to do in order to constantly improve. At this level we may even realise that we need to unlearn certain things in order to find new and better ways of doing the things we have previously done. For me, this is a level where significant meta-cognition takes place as we take time to reflect on our thinking and our actions.

Climbing the competency ladder is something that we all do as we go through a learning process. As educators, it is important for us to be aware of this in terms of developing our own skills, and it is also important for us to detect where a student might be in their own learning in order that we can best support them. We can also introduce the levels to students of different ages using appropriate language that best fits their present level of cognitive development.

Small things lead to big changes

Developing a mindset for success in a school will require many slight adjustments to current practice. Each of the small things we do, when combined, can lead to significant change. The following challenge illustrates how apparently small changes can build something that is enormous and, in this particular case, astronomical! You can use this with students as a way of giving them the message about how seemingly small learning steps taken through deliberate practice can lead them towards developing significant mastery.

Here's the challenge. If you were to take an average piece of printer paper it will very likely be around one-tenth of a millimetre in thickness (using the common 80 gsm variety). How thick would the paper be if you could fold it over once (this would double the thickness), then twice (this would now be four times the thickness of the original paper), then 10 times, then 20 times, then 30 times, then 50 times, and finally 100 times? Rather than giving your answer in millimetres, centimetres, metres and so on, think of the height of the folded paper in terms of the objects around you – for example, the thickness of this book, the width of your hand, the height of a chair, the height of the classroom or whatever else you would like to use.

If you have never heard of this before the answers might surprise you. In the table below are the thicknesses, or heights, in millimetres, centimetres and metres as well as some comparisons.

Number of folds	Comparable object or thing (approximately)	Width of folded paper
1	Thicker paper!	0.2 mm
2	Thickness of card	0.4 mm
10	Width of a hand	10 cm
20	The height of the Elizabeth Tower (which houses Big Ben)	100 m
30	The outer limits of the atmosphere	100 km
50	The distance to the sun	100,000,000 km
100	The radius of the known universe	100,000,000,000,000,000,000,000 km!

If you struggled to come up with answers that are as apparently outrageous as these then it is no big surprise. But what might this tell us? Well, one interpretation could be that a small thing can make an enormous difference. And this is what you will find as you develop a mindset for success in your school. Like folding paper, you are likely to be making small changes that can lead to tremendous ultimate results. It is about a drip-feed approach, which I will refer to on a number of occasions in this book. As John Wooden is reputed to have said, 'It's the little details that are vital. Little things make big things happen.'

In *The Talent Code*, Daniel Coyle explains how one apparently slight detail can make a significant difference to the amount of time and effort that a group of students were prepared to put into their studies. To illustrate this he describes an experiment carried out by Dr Geoff Cohen and his colleague Gregory Walton which began with a group of Yale freshmen being given some magazine articles to read.[5] Before we look at this let me ask you this question: if you were given something to read about a particular person and you found that the person had

5   D. Coyle, *The Talent Code: Greatness Isn't Born. It's Grown* (New York: Bantam Books, 2009), pp. 10–11.

the same birthday as you, do you think this could in any way affect your behaviour? I guess a lot of us would say no. However, strange things can happen on a subconscious level when we pick up information, as Cohen and Walton found in this experiment. Let's take a look at what they discovered.

The articles that the freshmen students at Yale were given to read included a short description of a student named Nathan Jackson and the article was written in the first person. It described how Nathan had arrived at a college not knowing what career he had in mind but then found he had an interest in studying maths. From this he was able to take a position in a maths department at a university and he was very happy. The information about Nathan also included where he was born and his birth date. The researchers then did a little sneaky thing and altered Nathan's birth date to match the birth date of half of the students.

The next step was for the researchers to give the students some maths questions that included one particular problem that was insoluble. The researchers wanted to see what the attitude of the freshmen was towards the maths questions and their persistence in trying to solve the insoluble problem. Their findings were that the birthday-matched group were prepared to spend an incredible 65% longer on the insoluble problem and their attitude in general towards maths was far more positive. What's more, the students themselves had not realised that there had been any change in their approach. Rather than it happening on a conscious level, this was taking place very much in a subconscious way.

Coyle makes two key points which are, I believe, important for us to consider as educators in schools. The first is about belonging. Human beings have a need to feel that they belong in a group or community. This is the third level up in Maslow's hierarchy of needs pyramid (which we will look at in Chapter 8). The students with the same birthday as Nathan Jackson seemed to feel that they were like him, that they could relate to him and that there was some sense of belonging associated with him. And the fact that Nathan had started out at college not knowing what career path he was going to go along would no doubt have resonated with many of the students. So when he decided that maths was the path that he wanted to take, this seemed to influence the birthday-matched students to be subconsciously persuaded that maths was something that they too may feel inclined towards. The second point concerns subtlety. It seemed to be the case that the students were influenced by what they read, and associated themselves with Nathan, only because they did not think they were involved in an experiment.

So, relating this to developing mindsets of success in your school, my suggestions are as follows:

- For belonging it is important that each and every child should believe that they have the capacity to achieve great things, if they are prepared to put in effort and deliberate practice and demonstrate persistence. We want all of them to feel that they are part of this philosophy in the school. Therefore, any discrimination between them must be actively avoided, and included in this is any labelling that we might associate with the children we teach.

- In terms of subtlety, we need to use our imagination in order to think about the kinds of messages that we can deliver to students about their potential and the importance of having a growth mindset which the students receive without them necessarily being fully aware that we are giving out these messages. This does not mean that we should not also talk openly at other times about the importance of growth mindsets and all that this involves. In fact, this is very important for us to do as well, as the students need to be aware of how they can work on growth mindsets themselves.

Another experiment that Coyle mentions was carried out by Gary McPherson who studied 157 randomly selected young children as they chose and then started to learn a musical instrument.[6] Some of these went on to become fine musicians and some faltered. The students were asked one simple question before they started learning to play their instrument: 'How long do you expect to keep playing this instrument: through this year, through primary school, through high school or for the rest of your life?' The answers were taken and compared with how well the students learned and how often they practised. What do you think they found?

Well, the first thing was not too surprising and correlates with what we know about deliberate practice. This was that the more the students practised (deliberately), the faster they got better. The second finding was not so obvious but,

6   Coyle, *The Talent Code*, p. 102.

perhaps, understandable. This was that the students who had made a lifelong commitment to playing their musical instrument also got better faster. In fact, it was found that with the same amount of practice, the long-term commitment group significantly outperformed the short-term commitment group by 400%! The third finding is, at least initially, the most surprising. This was that the long-term commitment group were able to practise for a shorter period of time than the short-term commitment group and still make faster progress. (Here 20 minutes of practice per week of the long-term group was compared with 90 minutes of practice of the short-term group.) You might want to be careful how you tell students about this!

The evidence seems to strongly suggest that:

> High levels of deliberate practice + long-term commitment = speediest learning

Their success seemed to have little to do with the skills they started out with, but rather with what we might refer to as 'attitude'.

It seems to be the case that when people have a long-term commitment, they see the thing that they are endeavouring to achieve as part of who they are. It is part of their identity and makes them more dedicated to the cause. In addition, it helps their RAS to subconsciously do a lot of work to support them. Those people who are doing something because their parents or teachers are insisting that this is 'good for them' are likely to react negatively, with lower levels of deliberate practice and long-term commitment. If they feel coerced into doing something, they lack a sense of ownership and, even if not consciously, they will react against this in an adverse way. Once we start to think about this it feels like common sense. However, for many of us it still remains *uncommon practice*. What is common, however, is to hear people say things like:

> I will never be good at this.
>
> I could never be good at maths – I just haven't got what it takes.
>
> I can't draw for my life!
>
> No one in my family was very bright, so what chance have I got?

And so it goes on. However, the evidence suggests that it is not inherent skills that we need but rather the correct attitude. Or, in other words, with the correct (growth) mindset we can surprise ourselves and others with what we can achieve. Providing this message of hope to all our students can help to stimulate in them the endurance to stick with a task and to see it with a long-term perspective. And we can help them further by emphasising the following:

- Encourage students to adopt a 'can do' attitude. We need to be relentless in this respect, not allowing students to talk themselves down with comments like, 'I'm just hopeless at this.' We don't give false information, but nor do we simply provide apparently comforting comments like, 'Oh yes you can. You are clever enough.' The student won't accept this comment and it serves them no good. They need to be told the facts, including our belief that they can succeed if they put the effort into the work and show real determination.

- Get students to focus on *when* they will achieve their target and not on *how* they will do it. The how will follow once they have a goal or vision of where they want to go, and when they aim to get there. We can emphasise that success will be determined by stickability. Lingering on thoughts about whether they have the skills to succeed will not help the student.

One final experiment to mention here involved a group of Dutch people who were asked to list the characteristics of trouble-making soccer fans. Another group were asked to list the characteristics of professors. They were then asked to play *Trivial Pursuit*. Surprisingly, those people who had focused on the characteristics of professors were able to answer more general knowledge questions than those who had been asked to list the characteristics of trouble-making soccer fans.[7] This once again illustrates how influential everything we do and say in the classroom can be.

In this chapter we have seen how deliberate practice leads on to long-term success, and how all learning involves climbing the ladder of competence up to the highest level of reflective competence. In addition we have looked at how a series of small steps can set in motion something that is magnificent. We need to be aware that all the small things we do in a classroom will impact in some way on the development of the students. At the same time, we need to be giving the students constant

7   S. Lilienfeld, *50 Great Myths of Popular Psychology: Shattering Widespread Misconceptions about Human Behavior* (Chichester: Wiley-Blackwell, 2010), p. 249. See also A. Dijksterhuis and A. van Knippenberg, The relation between perception and behavior, or how to win a game of *Trivial Pursuit*, *Journal of Personality and Social Psychology*, 74 (1998), 865–877.

feedback about the incremental growth that comes about through their willingness to constantly push themselves a little further out of their comfort zones. The more they do this, the more they will fail, and the more they fail, the more they will learn – and so make steady progress up the ladder of competence.

In the next chapter we will see how Carol Dweck's assertion that mindsets make a real difference to the progress of students in our schools is supported by the meta-research carried out by John Hattie.

Chapter 4
Support from other research

Visible learning

In 2009, Professor John Hattie's *Visible Learning* was published and provided us with a very important insight into what actually works in improving children's learning in schools.[1] John Hattie, and his team at the University of Auckland, New Zealand, carried out over 800 meta-analyses relating to the achievement of school-aged students. In other words, they collected mountains of data on different interventions in schools and tried to find out which of these strategies had the biggest impact on student learning. So Hattie's research is what is called meta-research, or research of the research. In total, his conclusions are based on the analysis of findings from over 50,000 educational studies across the world involving many millions of students. The *TES* sensationally claimed that *Visible Learning* 'reveals teaching's Holy Grail'.[2]

Hattie's work represents the largest ever collection of evidence-based research into what actually works in schools to improve learning (as well as those things that don't improve learning). Examples of the kinds of things that were analysed include homework, class size, student–teacher relationships, formative evaluation, teacher credibility, teacher expectations, classroom management and matching style of learning, along with many other factors that make up a total of 150 influences. Hattie was then able to allocate to each of these an 'effect size', which represents the impact that each of these influences has on students' learning. The 150 influences could then be placed into a table, with the influence ranked number one being the factor that has the greatest impact on student learning. The top

....

1   J. Hattie, *Visible Learning* (London: Routledge, 2009).

2   W. Mansell, Research reveals teaching's Holy Grail, *TES* (21 November 2008). Available at: https://www.tes.com/news/tes-archive/tes-publication/research-reveals-teachings-holy-grail.

influence turned out to be 'student expectations'. (Note: Hattie's work is ongoing and this stated top influence was determined at the time of writing.)

Hattie also observed that learning involves 'deliberate practice', rehearsal, error, re-teaching, listening, trying, exploring and so on. It is not easy. Although we may consider the influence of ability, talent and intelligence in human learning, these in themselves are not enough. Investment of time, energy, structured tuition and personal effort are all required if mastery in any particular field is to be attained. These findings are, of course, in direct alignment with the messages in this book, and in particular the findings of Carol Dweck and her work concerning mindsets. If student expectations (in other words, their expectations that with hard work and dedication they have a tremendous chance to succeed in their studies) are so important, as both Hattie and Dweck have established, then it seems clear to me that, as educators, we must do all we can to positively influence the expectations of all the students we teach.

For those who ask how we can possibly do this, we now have an answer: to work on the mindsets of students and to encourage them to adopt a growth mindset. Many ways of doing this can be found in this book, but none of these are one-off or even multiple activities, which once completed can be thought of as saying that we have 'done mindsets'. Because what we need in any school is a culture which embraces a mindset for success. This takes time, vigilance and dedication.

Professor John Hattie is a modern day benevolent Monty Hall!

When I am talking about Hattie's work in training sessions with staff, I usually say that 'Professor John Hattie is a modern day benevolent Monty Hall'! To begin with, and understandably, most people haven't got a clue what I'm talking about. So, I tell them the following story with the associated, and rather interesting, problem. The idea here is to get people to think about how so much of what we do in classrooms is down to guesswork.

Monty Hall was the host of the game show called *Let's Make a Deal*, which initially ran on US television from 1968 to 1977. The show invited contestants to guess behind which of three doors a prize was hidden. In the famous 'Monty Hall problem' (which is similar to the 'three prisoners problem' which preceded it), there is a car behind one of the doors and goats behind each of the other two doors.

Imagine that you are one of the contestants and you are asked to choose one door from the three. We will call the three doors A, B and C. Monty Hall knows which door the star prize of a brand new car is positioned behind.

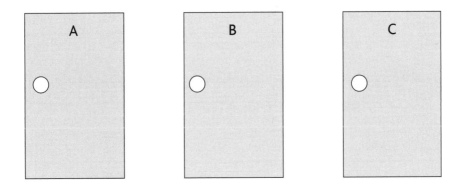

Let us suppose that you choose door A. Once you have done this, Monty then does you a big favour and opens one of the other two doors to reveal a goat. (Remember, at least one of the other two doors also has a goat behind it.) Suppose this is door B. He then offers you the possibility of changing to door C or sticking with door A. The car could be behind either of these two doors. What do you do? Think about this for yourself and decide on what you would do before looking at the answer below.

I assume that we will all agree that you have a one-in-three chance of initially choosing the star prize. And many (perhaps most) people will say that once Monty has opened one of the other two doors it makes no difference whether you change or not. They will say that you have a one-in-two chance that the car will be behind either A or C. Wrong! The answer is that you should change to door C if you want to increase your chance of winning (you never know, a new programme based on this format could be introduced on to present day TV!). Sticking with door A will give you your original one-in-three chance of winning. Moving to door C will give you a two-in-three chance of winning. This may seem completely counterintuitive but it is correct.

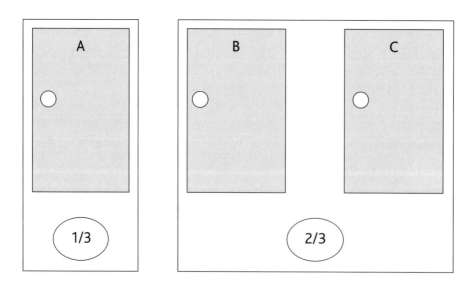

Think about it this way. Choosing any door at the start, in this case we chose door A, gives you a one-in-three chance of winning. Therefore the other two doors have collectively a two-in-three chance of the star prize being behind one of them. If at the start you were given the option of being able to choose just one door or two, you would of course take the two door option. So, rather than choosing just door

A (with a one-in-three chance of winning) you would take both B and C (with a two-in-three chance of winning). It's a no-brainer. The fact that door B is revealed to have a goat behind it simply shifts the two-in-three chance of winning the car over to door C. (I know, it's still rather confusing for most of us![3])

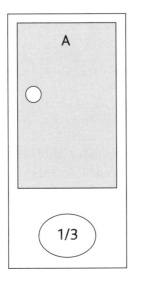 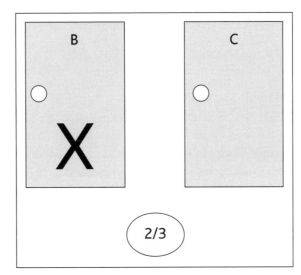

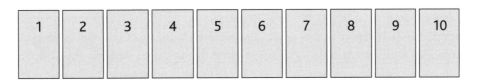

You still have a 2/3 chance of winning the star prize
if you move over to this side and door C

You may still not be convinced about the logic that lies behind the Monty Hall problem. However, I am going to take this one step further and ask you to imagine that there are 10 doors with the star prize being behind just one of them and goats behind each of the other nine. This time they are numbered from 1 to 10.

1	2	3	4	5	6	7	8	9	10

....

3   If you want to watch a very entertaining and fun video about this starring Alan Davies and
    Oxford mathematics professor Marcus Du Sautoy, then visit: https://www.youtube.com/
    watch?v=o_djTy3G0pg.

Again, for simplicity, let us suppose you choose door 1. You will agree that you have a one-in-ten chance of this being the door with the star prize. Therefore there is a nine-in-ten chance of the star prize being behind one of the other nine doors.

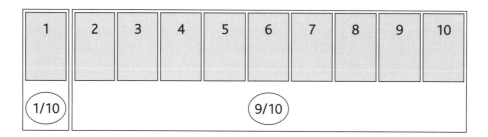

Suppose Monty Hall opens doors 2 to 9 revealing that each one has a goat behind it. He kindly gives you the option again to either stick with door 1 or to move to door 10. What do you do? Well, as we have seen, if you want to improve your chances of winning the car then you have to move to door 10 which itself now has a nine-in-ten chance of being the prize door.

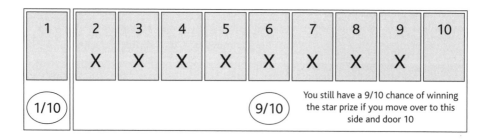

But how does this have relevance to what we do in our classrooms? Well, knowing what to choose that might affect the learning of our students out of the myriad of options available to us as teachers can seem like an impossibility. This is particularly the case if we are largely guessing or working on beliefs without any evidence about the things that make a difference. It is a bit like trying to guess the door with the prize behind it in the Monty Hall problem. But, remember, Monty does us a great favour by telling us how many of the doors do not have the star prize behind them and therefore we should not choose them.

In the world of education, I liken Professor John Hattie to the very benevolent Monty Hall! Through the findings from his meta-research, he has given us a great insight into what actually works in schools to improve learning. So rather than it being a gamble (or trying to guess the door with the star prize), we can focus on the things that really do make a difference. Out of the thousands of aspects that you could choose to focus on as a teacher, with the sincere hope that this will make a difference to the learning of your students, would you prefer to know which things really do have a big impact and those that have less impact, or would you prefer to guess? *Visible Learning* takes a lot of the guesswork out of the choices we make about how we might use our time in schools to improve the learning of the students. It also allows us to consider dropping some of the strategies that the research shows us are making little difference to our students.

It is not my intention here to consider Hattie's findings in any further detail, although I would strongly recommend that teachers in all schools should have an understanding of the key messages in *Visible Learning for Teachers*.[4] For the purposes of this book, and just to emphasise this once more, Hattie found that the top influence on the learning of students is their expectations, and their expectations will be positively influenced by them adopting a growth mindset. The more we can encourage students to adopt a belief that they can achieve a great deal, if they are prepared to commit themselves to the effort that is required to do this, the more likely it is that they will indeed learn more from their school experience. This apparently very simple message should be central to all that we do in schools. The next chapter will look at a variety of factors that influence the effectiveness of the mindset messages that we hear in our classrooms and around our schools.

....

4   Hattie, *Visible Learning for Teachers*.

Chapter 5
Using our heads

Leading on the mindset change

It is important that someone in the school takes on the key role of leading on mindsets. In the different schools in which I have worked, this has been taken on by one of a number of people. The head teacher or principal is the obvious person. If you are a head then you have the authority to place great importance and emphasis on the development of a constructive growth mindset culture. If you, as a head teacher, decide to delegate the leadership of the project to another person, it's important that they are given the authority and ownership for how the project is developed, with the head having an oversight but not telling the other person how to carry out the work. Ideally, the mindset for success project should be included in the school development plan and locked into both the mission and the vision of the school.

Using your RAS and teaching others how to use theirs

The RAS is an important part of the brain that adults in the school need to be aware of because it can support the messages we deliver concerning mindsets and enable us to discover many things that can support our work on mindsets. It helps in terms of alerting us to those things we believe to be important and therefore it assists us in achieving our goals. The RAS also acts like a filter: it allows important information through from the sensory organs and delivers this to the conscious mind. If you were to pay attention to all the information coming in from your senses then you would go crazy. The RAS is located at the top of the spinal column and extends upwards about 2 inches. It is about the size of a little finger.

All effective leaders know that having a very clear vision of what they want to achieve is fundamental to their ultimate success. Once we know what we want to achieve, then our RAS will support us to filter and block out information that doesn't match what we are looking for and allow through information that will support the achievement of our goals or vision. Astonishingly, we can eliminate information that is right in front of us if we believe it is not important. Naturally, all of this happens unconsciously, otherwise we would be operating in a mightily slow way – in fact, this would simply make our ability to function at all impossible.

The more we know what we want, the better we will be able to spot things to help us achieve our goal. As a leader, part of our job is to continually ignite the RAS of each individual we work with, so they will then be on the lookout for possibilities and opportunities and not for failure. Whether we focus on success or failure, we will be drawn towards it like a magnet. How we see things reflects who we are as individuals and, indeed, as a school society. This is why a powerful school vision is so important: it helps us to focus on what we believe are the most important elements. Our task is to make the vision so powerful that our own RAS, and the RAS of all members of the school, will not only be set to see the school the way that we want it to be, but it will also support us in progressively moving towards the way we want it to be. This creates a cascade or avalanche effect, but in order to keep it working it is essential that it is uppermost in the minds of everyone in the school.

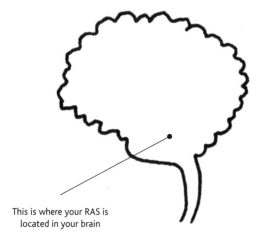

This is where your RAS is located in your brain

Using affirmations

I sometimes ask people in my audiences to put their hand up if they ever talk to themselves. In general everyone will raise their hands, but occasionally there will be the odd person who sits with a quizzical look on their face, pondering on whether they do indeed ever talk to themselves! Of course, we all do, and it is probably true to say that if one of our close friends ever said to us the sort of things we sometimes say to ourselves about ourselves then they would not remain one of our close friends for very long. We can be very tough on ourselves and we may think that this does not necessarily matter. After all, isn't everyone critical about themselves a lot of the time? The truth is that I don't know, but what I do know is that every time we tell ourselves something this idea or message is stored in our brain, just as each new piece of information or knowledge is stored through the connections created between our neurons.

> A man is literally *what he thinks*, his character being the complete sum of all his thoughts.
>
> James Allen[1]

We can control our thoughts if we wish to, and this deliberate control can impact on our brain and its physical structure. The brain is impressionable, so if we want our brain to support us then we need to feed it with helpful thoughts, just as our body needs to be fed with healthy food. If we don't do this then we cannot expect our brain to function well for us. We are, in effect, a manifestation of the thoughts we put into our minds. Now, at one level we could leave the whole process of what we put into our minds to chance. But this is like saying we have no choice about what we eat and put into our bodies. A completely different approach is to provide ourselves with a nourishing diet of positive thoughts that support our growth and the attainment of our goals. Therefore, we can have a deliberately healthy thought-diet to complement a deliberately healthy food-diet. And these deliberate thoughts are often referred to as affirmations.

....

1   J. Allen, *As a Man Thinketh* (1902). Available at: http://www.gutenberg.org/files/4507/4507-h/4507-h.htm.

Affirmations provide a way for us to train our brain to perform in a healthy and constructive way. The more we repeat certain positive thoughts or affirmations, the stronger the connections in our brain associated with these thoughts become, and the more our subconscious mind is able to use these to carry out actions without us having to consciously think about them. What we have stored in our brains motivates the actions we carry out. For example, if we tell ourselves that we tend to get nervous when we speak in front of an audience, then when we want to make a good impression with our first speech to a large group of parents we are very likely to act out being nervous. The thoughts we have stored by neuronal connections in our brain will, to a large extent, influence the experience we have of the world around us as well as the actions we take.

Just to be clear, an affirmation is self-talk made up from the words we speak out loud or, more often, privately to ourselves. Some of the things we say to ourselves can have a very beneficial impact, but unless we are careful we can also say things that can be highly destructive. If we don't take control of our self-talk then we can find that, inadvertently, it can act against our own best interests. The process of affirmations that we are going to use here will enable our self-talk to be wholly positive and support us in what we want to achieve every day, as well as with our long-term aspirations, goals and vision. So, it is not a question of whether to use affirmations or not: we all use them all of the time whether we consciously decide to do so or otherwise. We need to decide whether we want to use our self-talk in a way that allows our conscious mind to randomly feed good and bad affirmations into our subconscious mind without us monitoring them. This is frankly the easier and lazier way but it can have unpredictable and dangerous consequences. Alternatively we can decide to use affirmations in a way that supports us. This requires us to supervise the thoughts we allow ourselves to think (and say) and thereby feed into our subconscious mind. The more we take on control of the thoughts we feed through to our subconscious mind, the more this will become a habit and second nature.

Most of us, at one time or another, will have been hurt by what somebody has said to us. At the same time, we will all have been motivated at some time by what somebody has said to us. We cannot deny the power of words. What we were told and accepted as we grew up will have become part of what we consider ourselves to be. Comments by others sink into our subconscious minds and we will often repeat these statements to ourselves without even being aware of it. Some of these observations will give us a real buzz; others could make us feel very bad. In my early days of teaching I once asked a colleague why he seemed so confident and self-assured in almost any situation. He told me it was because when he was young he was told by those around him that they believed in his potential to do things, almost anything, very well – and he believed them. I have no idea whether the individuals who nurtured his early childhood systematically and consciously tried to give him positive feedback, but the consequence was that he had a very high self-image, self-esteem and self-efficacy, all of which served him very well. He was very much liked by staff and pupils in the school, and he was in no way arrogant. Although I did not know it at the time, I now realise that he had a powerful growth mindset.

On the other hand, I have known many people, both young and old, who were only fed a diet of negativity and, perhaps unsurprisingly, they have gone on to feel negative themselves about their life chances in this challenging and, as they see it, unfriendly world. But it doesn't have to stay this way. Once we understand how the things we feed into our mind impact on our behaviour, which then impacts on our success, we can do something about it. No one has to continue to live a life where they feel powerless or on the 'effect' side of the equation. We can all grow to be more and more on the 'cause' side of the equation, if we choose to do so. We *can* take control and we *can* deliver this message to all the pupils that we teach.

This does not mean that we can remove from our subconscious minds the experiences and messages we have been told by other people. Rather, we can nourish our mind with positive statements about ourselves that, over time, balance and then exceed any negatives that exist. We can then become the kind of person we want to be. Athletes, for example, use the power of affirmations (or self-talk) and visualisation to great effect. These ideas exploit our knowledge of how our minds and the neural biology in our brains work, and it now has sound scientific support.

Anyone who thinks that affirmations do not work for them should beware. The fact is that if you don't think the formal process of affirmations will work then you will be 100% right. The process will not work for anyone who believes this – in effect, they have created a very powerful affirmation which will ensure that affirmations simply won't work for them! However, we are all using affirmations whether we would like to or not because you and I are constantly talking to ourselves. Consciously using affirmations is simply a way of making our self-talk work for us rather than against us. By using affirmations our subconscious mind will begin to produce new beliefs and new behaviours that support us in life.

There is a way of carrying out the affirmation process that will work most powerfully for you. The steps are simple but they are essential if you want to have great success as quickly as possible with the process. The six principles are as follows.

Principle 1: Always use the present tense

Using affirmations in the present tense is the way that we will get most energy from them. It gives us the feeling that the goal we are aiming for has already been achieved – and feelings are of critical importance in the success of affirmations.

> This statement will not work so well: 'I am going to ...' This gives a sense of hope but no certainty.
>
> This will work: 'I am now ...' It provides certainty and it gives a clear message to your subconscious mind.

A student might say, for example, 'I am going to put in lots of effort.' They may believe this but it will not work as powerfully as, 'I get real pleasure from always putting a lot of effort into my history assignment.' This statement will work a real treat.

A lot of people find it a challenge to state affirmations in the present tense. They tell me that it is hard for them to say that the world is a particular way when they perceive it differently at that moment. If you feel this as well then you must either drop this belief and trust in the power of affirmations or you can use a staged approach.

> The challenge is: 'I feel nervous in meetings.'
>
> A direct affirmation to help to overcome this could be: 'I feel confident in meetings.'

This may seem too much of a challenge for someone to say initially, therefore a staged approach would be to say:

Stage 1: 'Every day I feel more and more confident in meetings and see myself speaking with greater and ever increasing clarity.'

As this begins to take effect the affirmation could become:

Stage 2: 'I get a real feeling of satisfaction from confidently speaking in meetings and seeing the respect people have for me.'

You can teach this two stage process to your students as well.

Principle 2: Keep it goal oriented

You must always keep your affirmations positive. Affirmations should be wholly focused on what we want, not what we want to get rid of! If we include in an affirmation what we don't want (even by making it clear that we don't want it), our subconscious mind will focus on this. Let's look at an example.

A goal you have: 'I want to lose weight.'

A negative affirmation could be: 'I want to be less fat than I am now.'

This affirmation has two negatives so it won't work to support us:

1. It is not in the present tense (see principle 1).

2. Its focus is on a negative – being 'fat'.

The impact of the second negative is that your subconscious mind will focus on fat, fat, fat, and not on the desired state that you want. The affirmation needs to focus on your goal.

The following is an example of the way an affirmation can support you.

Positive affirmation: 'I have a very warm feeling about now weighing X stone and seeing myself in the mirror wearing size Y clothes.'

Clearly, both affirmations point to the same end result – weight loss. The impact they have on you, however, will be completely different. The positive affirmation provides you with great imagery, feeling and energy in support of your goal of losing weight.

Principle 3: Use VAK (visual, auditory, kinaesthetic) language

Note here that the affirmation above contains visual (seeing), auditory (speaking) and kinaesthetic (feeling) aspects (the visual part is 'seeing myself in the mirror wearing size Y clothes', the auditory part is satisfied by the fact that we speak the affirmation to ourselves and the kinaesthetic part concerns the 'warm feeling' that is generated). You may not include these three aspects of our senses in every affirmation, but the more you can, the more powerful the affirmation will be.

In this way you will make your affirmations resonate with you. (If you want, you could also use gustatory (taste) and olfactory (smell) words as well.) The words you use should enable you to experience the goal that you now have in the strongest way possible. As you read out an affirmation ensure that you experience the state in strong VAK terms.

The affirmation in principle 2 above was:

> 'I have a very warm feeling about now weighing X stone and seeing myself in the mirror wearing size Y clothes.'

You could add a little more auditory language in here as well so that the affirmation becomes:

> 'I have a very warm feeling about now weighing X stone and I say to myself when I look in the mirror "Wow, you look good in those size Y clothes."'

Note: It is not always necessary to add auditory words because the affirmation itself makes use of words.

Principle 4: Talk about yourself

You make affirmations for yourself. This is not being selfish: if you want to achieve things in this world that will support you on your journey through life, then you must get things to work as well for yourself as possible in the first instance. You cannot directly affect the behaviour of other people through affirmations. You must therefore use 'I' in your statements. When you are operating as effectively as you can, then you will be in the best position to support those around you.

Principle 5: Make sure your affirmation follows the SMARTER criteria for setting goals

SMARTER is an acronym that stands for *specific, measurable, achievable, realistic, time bound, energising* and *rewarding*. We should always check that the goals we set ourselves satisfy these criteria. If we look at the S for specific criteria we can use an example of a goal of getting fit. The following affirmations may be used to support us in achieving this goal.

Affirmation 1: 'I exercise regularly.'

Affirmation 2: 'I exercise twice a week.'

Affirmation 3: 'I exercise twice a week on Monday and Saturday.'

Affirmation 4: 'I go to the gym and swim twice a week on Monday and Saturday from 1 p.m. to 2 p.m.'

As the affirmations become more specific (going from 1 to 4) they grow in strength. The more specific we can be, the more we are likely to keep to the affirmation. Just saying 'I exercise regularly' could involve going for a jog for ten minutes once a year! We would have fulfilled the affirmation and our subconscious mind would be satisfied with having done its job!

Principle 6: Make it short and hit the sweet spot

Your subconscious mind will tend to deal most effectively with messages that are succinct. Your conscious mind will also be able to deal best with messages that are not too long and are easy to remember. You need to repeat affirmations on a regular basis for them to have a long-term impact on your subconscious mind, therefore try to make affirmations that are short and hit the 'sweet spot' – that is, aim for them to have the greatest impact for the least effort.

In terms of developing a mindset for success in your school you can use the affirmation process to support you in the actions that you take. I teach this affirmation process to the adults I work with in schools and some have found it to be very useful in their private life as well as their working life. The more we repeat affirmations to ourselves, the more effective they become, and in the longer term they develop into the natural way that we operate. Examples of affirmations that people have created in training sessions include:

'I always praise effort and not the child.'

'I love encouraging children to experiment and take risks.'

'I remind children every day that IQ is not fixed.'

'Twice in every lesson I give examples of how mistakes have led on to great learning.'

The affirmation process is a valuable tool to introduce to children as a way of helping them to take control of their thinking.

The brain and what we need to know

The following information about the brain is not meant to be a thorough analysis of how this complex organ works. There are many excellent books and information on the Internet for those of us who are interested in studying in detail the information that neuroscience is now revealing about the inner workings of the brain. Rather, the ideas about the brain that are touched on here are those which I have found to be useful in terms of promoting a mindset for success in schools.

We live in truly exciting times in terms of education. And, of course, it is challenging as well. It is my belief that we are on the cusp of some remarkable advances in the way that we teach because of our ever-increasing understanding of the brain. In the past 30 years, it is claimed, we have discovered more about the secrets of the brain than we have known about for the past 3,000 years. These findings will play a big part in how we educate students both now and in the future, or at least they should. The brain is the organ that allows us to experience the world in our own unique way and enables us to achieve things in our lives.

As educators, there is the potential for us to use the rich information known about the brain to improve learning, yet in general, across the profession, our knowledge of neuroscience could be better. The following is a summary of some of the key aspects of the brain that impact most on the creating of a mindset for success culture in schools. In Chapter 10 I will explain some of the exciting ways to demonstrate certain aspects of the brain to pupils. Some of you might be asking why we need to understand how the brain works or inform children about how their brains work. Well, the research tells us that the more pupils understand the working of the brain, the more they will be able to appreciate the control they have over how it functions and the way that we can use it in a growth mindset way. So here we go – hold on to your seats and feel your brain grow!

Key thought 1

A newborn baby's brain weighs around 350–400 g, so slightly less than 1 pound which is around 450 g. By the time we are adults our brain will have more than tripled in size to around 3 pounds.

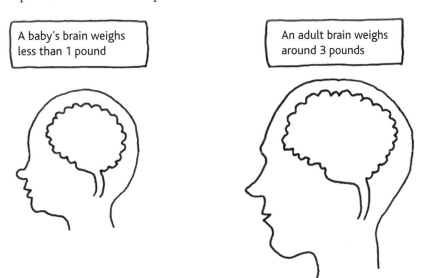

A baby's brain weighs less than 1 pound

An adult brain weighs around 3 pounds

Key thought 2

The brain is around 2% of the adult body weight, but around 20% of our blood supply feeds the brain. This means that 20% of the energy (calories) we consume are used up by the brain, which is more than the energy used by any other organ. Our brains are hungry!

Key thought 3

Researchers have now confirmed that the human brain is plastic in that it develops in response to learning and experience. This is often referred to as neuroplasticity. In general, neuroplasticity occurs in the brain when life begins (and the immature brain goes through a process of organising itself), when an individual suffers a brain injury (and the brain finds a way to compensate for lost functions), and as we learn things throughout our lives.

Dr Pascale Michelon has discovered that areas in the brains of experts which process their specific type of skill can grow.[2] An example of this is London taxi drivers who have a larger hippocampus than London bus drivers.[3] The reason for this can be explained by the fact that taxi drivers carry an internal map of London in their minds as they travel around a multitude of potential different routes, whereas bus drivers usually follow the same route each day. The hippocampus is the part of the brain that deals with these complex spatial configurations.

Plasticity can also be observed in the brains of people who are bilingual,[4] as well as in the brains of musicians when compared to the brains of non-musicians. When professional musicians, who might practice for at least one hour per day, are

---

2   P. Michelon, Brain plasticity: how learning changes your brain, *SharpBrains* (26 February 2008). Available at: http://sharpbrains.com/blog/2008/02/26/brain-plasticity-how-learning-changes-your-brain/.

3   E. Maguire, K. Woollett and H. Spiers, London taxi drivers and bus drivers: a structural MRI and neuropsychological analysis, *Hippocampus*, 16(12) (2006), 1091–1101.

4   A. Mechelli, J. Crinion, U. Noppeney, J. O'Doherty, J. Ashburner, R. Frackowiak and C. Price, Neurolinguistics: structural plasticity in the bilingual brain, *Nature*, 431(7010) (2004), 757.

compared to amateur musicians and non-musicians it has been discovered that there is a distinct difference in the volume of grey matter in several brain areas. This was highest in professional musicians, intermediate in amateur musicians and lowest in non-musicians.[5] This very much links with the idea of deliberate practice.

The very clear message that we can give to our students is that learning truly does transform the brain, even in a physical sense. As teachers we need to be aware of this ourselves, and inform students that we teach about the amazing capacity of the human brain to change structurally. A simple way of describing this process to students is given below.

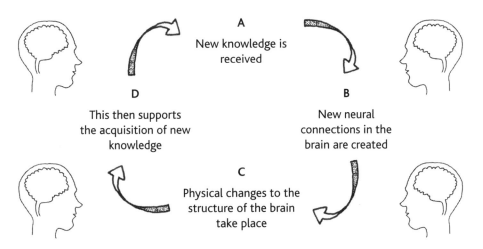

A
New knowledge is received

B
New neural connections in the brain are created

C
Physical changes to the structure of the brain take place

D
This then supports the acquisition of new knowledge

In some respects, we could say that our software (mind) affects our hardware (brain), and the hardware also impacts on the software. The growth of one supports the growth of the other. Our thinking creates changes in the structure of our brain that supports our ability to think even better in the future. There is a symbiotic relationship that is fundamental to our growth and existence as human beings. One of the great assumptions of neuroscience for many years was that the brain 'created' our mental processes and shaped the mind. It was a one-way process. We now know that there is in fact a two way process taking place, with our

5   C. Gaser and G. Schlaug, Brain structures differ between musicians and non-musicians, *NeuroImage*, 13(6) (2001), 1168.

mental processes changing the structure of our brains as well as our brains forming our mental processes. This is perhaps the most important message to pass on to our students in order to help them develop a growth mindset. We can literally restructure our brains to become cleverer all the time. How far we can take this is unknown, but great fun to play around with!

Key thought 4

In the foetus we grow 250,000 brain cells (neurons) each minute. By the time we are born we have over 20 billion. Most people will say that we have 100 billion neurons (cells) in our adult brain, but a more accurate number appears to be 86 billion. Neurons can make up to 10,000 connections with other neurons. Scientists have known for some decades that learning and memory manifest themselves in the physiological bridging of synapses. (Synapses are the gaps between neurons that are bridged by an axon and chemically or electrically link with a dendrite from another neuron.) These connections represent our learning. This learning may be the knowledge we have acquired as well as our habits, beliefs, attitudes and expectations. And the more we work at something, the stronger our connections become. We cannot unlearn what we have learned (in other words, we can't snap the connections), but where we learn that a piece of information is false or a belief we have is not helping us any more, we can counterbalance the original information and connections with new information and beliefs − all, obviously, having their own associated connections.

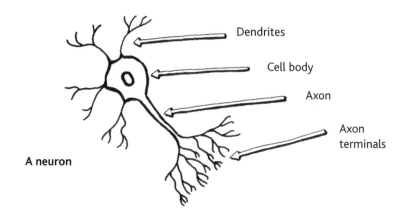

Dendrites

Cell body

Axon

Axon terminals

A neuron

Key thought 5

It is estimated that we transmit through our senses to our brain around 11 million signals or units of information per second. Astonishing, I think we would all agree. These are mostly through our eyes as we can see in the table below.

Sensory system	Bits per second
Eyes	10,000,000
Skin	1,000,000
Ears	100,000
Smell	100,000
Taste	1,000

However, the conscious mind only processes around 40 bits per second. To my own mind this is still a lot! We only take in what we think of as being important. This is something we need to be consciously aware of as teachers. The diagram below illustrates how this deletion impacts on what we experience in the world around us.

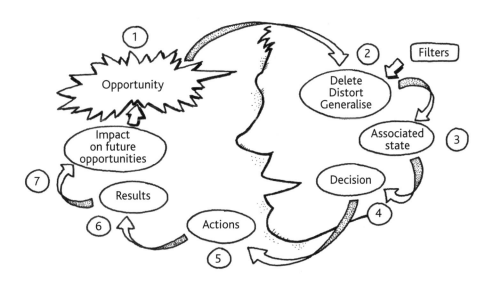

Let us work through the seven stages.

- Stage 1: An opportunity comes along for an individual.

- Stage 2: The question is not whether the opportunity is there but whether this individual will allow it through or block it out. Will it be included in the 40 bits of information allowed through or part of the 1,999,960 bits of information blocked out each second?[6] The majority of information will be deleted by the filters of our minds because it is viewed as unimportant. 'We hear and apprehend only what we already half know,' as Henry David Thoreau observed.[7] But the information that does get through can still be distorted, so we actually allow the details of the opportunity through but we interpret it in a certain way. For example, if a student feels they have been treated unfairly in the past by a male teacher in a primary school then they may, at least initially, distort the support given to them by another male teacher and think of it as unhelpful. This may also cause them to generalise about male teachers.

- Stage 3: Now the information that has been allowed through in its potentially distorted and generalised form puts us into a state which could be happy, sad, excited, angry and so on.

- Stage 4: As a result of this state we make a decision.

- Stage 5: This decision persuades us to take action.

- Stage 6: The action brings about certain results.

- Stage 7: These results are stored in our brain and manifest themselves mostly through our subconscious mind. They now form part of our world experience. This then impacts on the way we experience future experiences and opportunities in terms of the deletion, distortion and generalisation that goes on at stage 2.

....

6   See A. Dijksterhuis, (2004). Think different: the merits of unconscious thought in preference development and decision making, *Journal of Personality and Social Psychology*, 87(5), 586–598.

7   H. D. Thoreau, The Journal of Henry David Thoreau. In B. Torrey (ed.), *The Writings of Henry David Thoreau: Vol. XIII* (Boston, MA: Houghton Mifflin, 1906), pp. 77–78.

Key thought 6

In the past two million years the adult human brain has nearly tripled in size from just a little bigger than a present day baby's brain to the present day 3 pound adult brain.

These six facts about the brain form a starting point for discussion with students that should support them in adopting a growth mindset. Scientists today now tell us that the capacity for both lifelong learning and for our brains to develop throughout our lives is greater than we ever previously realised. It is no exaggeration to say that a brain science revolution has occurred. And alongside the brain we have its mysterious partner, the mind. We will now look at the way the mind functions, including both its conscious and subconscious parts.

The conscious and subconscious mind

The mind is often said to have two parts which we call the conscious and subconscious. It has become very clear that the subconscious mind plays a far greater part than the conscious mind in how we operate on a daily basis. The subconscious mind is where we make most of our decisions and where most of our potential for future achievement lies. Our subconscious mind operates at high speed, using our stored knowledge, memories, habits, attitudes, expectations and beliefs to help us function on autopilot. It is our subconscious mind that reveals much about our character. But just what is the mind? Philosophers have argued for thousands of years about this. It is generally agreed that the mind is not a physical entity but that the mind is involved in cognitive (mental) processes that enable the processes shown in the diagram to take place.

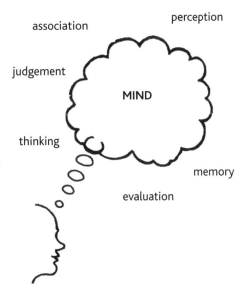

87

We usually split the mind into two distinct parts – the conscious mind and the subconscious mind. The diagram below illustrates the differences between the two parts.

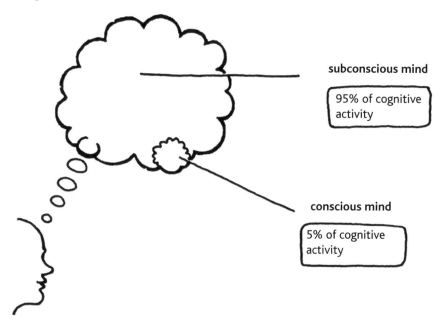

subconscious mind

95% of cognitive activity

conscious mind

5% of cognitive activity

Cognitive neuroscientists estimate that the conscious mind contributes only about 5% of our cognitive activity, and that 95% of our decisions, actions, emotions and behaviours are derived from the subconscious mind. This is why it is so important for us to be ever more aware of the information and beliefs that we are allowing ourselves to store in our brains. In effect, what we have stored in our brains drives 95% of what we do in an automatic, subconscious way. If we want to change some of the things that we do, then we need to store new things in our brain. And so, as educators, we need to appreciate that whatever our beliefs might be, they will influence what goes on in the classroom more than we might previously have imagined (as the Rosenthal experiment that we looked at in the introduction clearly demonstrated).

Research now supports what many of us may have suspected for some time – that is, the success of a teacher depends fundamentally on their own beliefs and the beliefs they generate in the students they teach. But my argument here is that the skills, attributes or characteristics, call them what you like, of great educators, are available for all of us to develop if (a) we are prepared to believe that change is possible, (b) we want to develop ourselves constantly and (c) we are prepared to spend the time required to try out new ideas and hone our skills.

Consciously using the subconscious

We want to deliver a message to the students that if they try they will always get better. We are role models for our students and as such we should demonstrate to them that we, ourselves, are constantly striving to improve. One way of doing this is to model the behaviour of the expert educators that can be found in most schools. The most important part of this involves finding out about their beliefs and values. Simply trying to copy their actions and behaviours may not be enough if we don't adjust our beliefs and values to correspond with these actions and behaviours. This analysis may take time and some might say that it is not possible for us to adjust the way we are. If by this people mean that it is impossible for a person to change their character or personality, then we must argue against this. Research is showing that, just as the brain is malleable or plastic, so is our character or personality.

Carol Dweck's *Mindset* is a book of hope for all of us, and I trust that this book also reinforces this hope. A growth mindset is a tale of success that we can all achieve if this is what we desire. For each of us our success will be both utterly unique and at the same time we will share common characteristics, qualities, skills and beliefs. We all need to be prepared, as we go through developing a mindset for success in schools, for some of our present beliefs to be challenged; those deep-seated beliefs are stored in our brains and direct the subconscious mind. Changing our beliefs is a real challenge for all of us. Once we hold a belief then we may think that this is 'part of us' and that changing the belief would involve taking away this part, almost like removing a physical part of our bodies. However difficult it may be to change a belief, this will always be necessary if we are to truly change a behaviour.

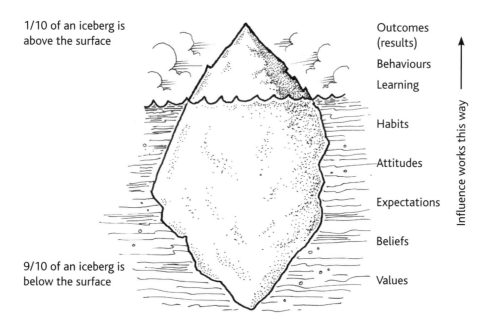

1/10 of an iceberg is above the surface

Outcomes (results)

Behaviours

Learning

Habits

Attitudes

Expectations

Beliefs

9/10 of an iceberg is below the surface

Values

Influence works this way

We are like the iceberg above. What is above the surface is fairly easy for us and others to know about. What lies below the surface is difficult even for us to be aware of sometimes, as it is largely a result of our subconscious mind at work. The outcomes (or results) we experience are dependent on our behaviours, which in turn are dependent on our learning. This is all relatively straightforward to witness and is above the metaphorical water level. However, our learning will depend on our habits, expectations and attitudes which will have been established within us over our lifetime. These depend on our beliefs and values, so to change outcomes we will need to change our beliefs (and values). Sometimes these might seem to be quite insignificant but they can make a big impact on the way that we operate.

Beliefs and values tend to merge into each other but the difference between them is important. Beliefs are like on/off switches. They are, in our minds, things that are for us true or false. Beliefs can change as we gain further information and knowledge. For example, as a child, you may have believed in the tooth fairy. The likelihood is that now you no longer do! You may have once believed that to clean paint brushes after using gloss paint you needed to use turpentine, whereas now you have been told that some newly developed paints can be cleaned up using soapy water. In general beliefs are not as difficult as values to change (though that tooth fairy one might have caused you some anguish!). However, values have a sense of right/wrong or good/bad about them – for example, you may value honesty and not be willing to give up this value. Our values and beliefs act as driving forces within us even though we will not be consciously aware of them at all times.

A lot of people imagine that the beliefs, habits and attitudes they have acquired during their journey through life largely cannot be changed. A basic premise of this book, and growth mindsets, is that this is not the case. Making sure that our beliefs, habits and attitudes all serve us well, both personally and professionally, is something that we cannot ignore, particularly if we want to pass this message on to our students. However, my observations are that these are not issues that are often discussed in schools. We have a choice in these matters: do we want to stay the way we are or do we want to change?

What we really want to encourage in our students is the inner desire to put in hours of deep focused (deliberate) practice that will enable them to master a skill. Of course, this is easier said than done. It requires a lot of energy and mental focus and it is tiring. All of us, teachers and students alike, will tend to make a deal with ourselves that goes something like:

Self 1: Do I really need to do this?

Self 2: Well, yes but I can get by without it. (This is likely to be true in most cases.)

Self 1: Okay then – maybe another time.

Daniel Coyle suggests that an individual has to be willing to suffer through the now, keeping in mind the later rewards.[7] We call this delayed gratification. This is what some of the children in Walter Mischel's famous marshmallow experiment were able to do.[8] In the 1960s and 1970s, Mischel carried out a fascinating series of experiments that involved 4-year-olds and marshmallows. The pre-school children were given one marshmallow but told that if they could refrain from eating this until the researcher returned to the room, they would be given a second marshmallow. The researcher then left the room for between 15 to 20 minutes. As you might expect, some children were able to hold out until the researcher

---

7   Coyle, *The Talent Code*.

8   W. Mischel, E. B. Ebbesen and A. R. Zeiss, Cognitive and attentional mechanisms in delay of gratification, *Journal of Personality and Social Psychology*, 21(2) (1972), 204–218.

returned while others were simply unable to withstand the temptation. Records were made of those children who were able to resist the temptation and those who were not. The same children were then revisited some 12 to 14 years later when they were in their adolescence.

The difference between those who had grabbed the marshmallow and those who had resisted it was startling. Now in their adolescence, those who had resisted temptation were more socially competent, more personally effective and had more self-assertiveness and confidence. They were more trustworthy and dependable, they were far better able to cope with the frustrations of life, they embraced challenges and pursued them rather than giving up when difficulties came along, and they took the initiative. All of these things can be associated with what we are striving to achieve by developing growth mindsets in our students. In addition, although a decade had passed, they were still able to delay the temptation of instant gratification in order to move powerfully towards their goals.

In stark contrast, the third of the children who had grabbed the marshmallow tended to have a less positive profile. For example, they had a tendency to be more stubborn and indecisive, to get easily frustrated, to think of themselves as being 'bad' or unworthy, they were prone to jealousy and envy, they overreacted to irritations by getting bad tempered, and they tended to get into arguments and fights. And it may not surprise us to learn that they were still unable to put off instant gratification.

When the same students were once again evaluated as they were leaving high school, it was found that those who had the highest level of deferred gratification also had significantly higher scores in their SAT tests. The characteristics of these 'grabbers' and 'deferred gratification' children are very aligned with those that we see in the 'fixed mindset' and 'growth mindset' children. It would have been very interesting to see if growth mindset training would have had any impact on the grabbers. Research evidence suggests that it could have supported them a great deal.

Employing coaching

The creation of a constructive culture with a mindset for success, where the language of a growth mindset is commonly spoken, can be supported by incorporating coaching into the school. In fact, I bring in coaching training as an integral part of establishing growth mindsets in the work I carry out with schools. Below, I will set out the reasons why I believe so strongly in the importance of coaching as an essential tool to support growth mindsets, what coaching is in terms of growth mindsets, and how to establish and use coaching in your school.

Why coaching?

First of all, let us look at why coaching is important in terms of mindsets and creating a mindset for success. Many schools talk a lot about coaching but fewer, in my experience, actually take coaching seriously – and the number one reason given for this is time. My response to this, perhaps controversially, is that the reason that schools don't have the time is that they don't do coaching! Clearly, there are a number of very important pragmatic things to consider. These include how to carry out the coaching, who to involve, where the coaching will take place, when it will take place, will there be formal and informal coaching, who leads on it, are certain people given extra time to do coaching, are the pupils to be trained as coaches and so on. Where coaching is tried and fails, it is often down to a poorly thought-out development plan. People are busy in schools, and unless they can see the purpose in putting effort into coaching, then they will understandably do something else. It takes time for schools to fully appreciate the benefits of coaching but when they do, they realise that all of their efforts have been worthwhile.

In the world of business, organisations such as PricewaterhouseCoopers report a six-to-one return on investment from coaching.[9] If schools get a return anything like this then the cost will have been worth it. Two of the fundamental reasons

---

9   Quoted in A. Leimon, F. Moscovici and G. McMahon, *Essential Business Coaching* (1st edn) (London: Routledge, 2005), p. 8.

why coaching adds to the successful implementation of a mindset for success in schools are:

1. It taps into potential. Coaching complements the philosophy of mindsets in that it looks at the possibilities that lie within people. I refer to it as a strengths focused model rather than a deficit model. It is about growth and progress.

2. A belief in the individual. A central element of coaching is the belief that the solution lies within the person being coached. In addition, a coach believes that with determination, deliberate practice and resilience, the limits of what any individual is able to achieve are indeterminable.

We can also look at the benefits that coaching brings to the pupils, the adults in the school and the whole school. First let us consider the pupils. Coaching pupils encourages them to make their own decisions, it improves their intrinsic motivation, it allows them to reflect on the very best learning strategies they might employ, it creates a resilient attitude, it nurtures a very constructive relationship between them and their peers and adults, it links success with effort, it improves their self-knowledge, it gives them an appreciation of their personal potential, and it enables them to see that setbacks are temporary and can be a real source of learning. All of these are, of course, essential skills and beliefs for students to develop in their journey to acquiring a growth mindset.

In terms of the benefits from a growth mindset that are acquired by adults in the school who themselves are being coached, this will clearly depend on the particular focus of the coaching. However, the benefits I have observed in teachers and other adults who have had the opportunity to be coached are that it encourages a reflective approach to their work, it improves their motivation, it supports effective teamworking, it improves job satisfaction, it supports a greater understanding of themselves and others, it instils a constructive approach to dealing with challenges, and it encourages creative thinking and risk taking. Again, all of these assist the development of growth mindsets in the school.

There are also significant benefits that come to the people doing the coaching. These include an understanding of the drives that motivate their colleagues and the pupils, development of the essential leadership skills of coaching, enhanced self-knowledge, increased communication skills, and the learning they get from having the privilege to coach other people through their challenges. And, unquestionably, the school itself will experience many benefits from investment in coaching, including improved academic standards, the creation of an ever more constructive and positive culture, better relationships between adults and pupils in the school, individuals taking on more responsibility for their own development (both staff and pupils), the school developing a collective achievement culture, and an openness to constantly looking for how to improve all aspects of the school and in particular teaching and learning. Once again, all of these things assist the development of a growth mindset culture.

What is coaching?

People are often initially confused about the difference between coaching and mentoring. Although there are overlaps in terms of the skills employed, coaching and mentoring are significantly different. Perhaps one of the most important distinctive features of coaching is that it is very much a strengths focused approach, whereas it may be argued that mentoring is more of a deficit model. By this I mean that coaching is seeking to explore and develop the abilities that lie within an individual, whereas mentoring might be looking to fill a gap in an individual's skills or knowledge. Both are very important, but it is essential to understand which one of these pathways to improvement we are taking. With coaching we truly believe that the person being coached (the coachee) has within themselves the answer to a challenge. We can see how much this links with the philosophy of growth mindsets.

A coach also aims to enable the coachee to become ever more independent, and in terms of the pupils this is a vital life skill. In addition, as educators and teachers we are then in a far more powerful position to be able to utilise our precious skills in order to bring about the greatest learning for the students, rather than having to spend a lot of time trying to almost force students to learn. Coaching can therefore be said to be nurturing intrinsic motivation within students (and indeed within adults) rather than having to resort to extrinsic motivational rewards to encourage them to commit to the work. Another important feature of coaching is that it is completely non-judgemental. It is not about being right or wrong, but rather it is used to explore options and for the coachee to decide on what they believe the best option to take might be. Linked with this, we are not directing the coachee towards a particular outcome that we have decided for them, but instead we want to empower them to choose what they want to do in order to achieve their goals.

How can I use coaching in my school?

If a school is thinking about developing coaching then the first thing that has to be considered is how to gain the knowledge that is required in order for individuals to be able to coach effectively. If you are in charge of coaching development then you might begin by researching and reading about coaching, learning about coaching from a colleague in your school who has themselves been trained as a coach or finding a training programme that satisfies the school's requirements. I have run coaching training programmes in schools that have varied from a one day course to something that has extended over a six month period and resulted in teachers in the school receiving a professional qualification from the Institute of Leadership and Management. My recommendation is that, if the school is serious about developing a mindset for success culture which is supported by a coaching approach, then a programme for training all staff in the school should be considered. This, of course, takes commitment and time, but the benefits of building internal capacity for developing children's mindsets, together with the sustainability to take this forward into the future growth of the school, are well worth the effort that needs to be put in at the outset.

The structure of coaching that is most popular, and the one that I use to train people in coaching, is called the GROW model. This provides a framework for any coaching session that is either formally or informally undertaken. The acronym GROW stands for *goal, reality, options* and *will*. Each of the four stages plays an important part in enabling the coachee to explore all aspects of the challenge they are facing and the end result they are seeking. The model works like this.

Goal

In the goal stage, the coach supports the coachee to have clarity about what they are trying to achieve. At first this may seem obvious but, by using powerful yet very simple questions, the coach encourages the coachee to think in a deep way about their goal. The more they understand this, the greater their attraction towards it will be. Their RAS will be fully activated to be on the lookout for ways of achieving the goal. There are many questions that we can ask the coachee and obviously some of these will depend on the situation. However, there are some brilliant and simple questions that can be used almost universally. These include:

● What exactly do you want to achieve in both the short term and long term?

● Where does this goal fit into your personal priorities in your life at present?

● What would you like to achieve by the end of this coaching session (or lesson)?

● Can you achieve what you want today in the time available (or in this lesson)?

● Is any part of it measurable? How will you measure it?

Reality

In the reality stage we help the coachee to explore where they are at the moment. It is hard for any of us to be able to know what steps we need to take towards our goal without having clarity about where we are at the moment. Whether we are working with a teacher who wants us to explore with them how they can ask growth mindset questions in their classroom, or we are ourselves working with an individual student in our classroom who is seeking to structure an English essay, it is very useful for them to be clear about their present situation. This is often called 'current reality' because it is simply where we are at the moment and in no way determines where we will be in the future, as long as we apply ourselves. This is a growth mindset message that we want to continually deliver to all of those around us. Useful questions for the reality stage include:

- What actions have you already taken (if any) to try to reach this goal?

- What have you learned from that?

- How would you rate your achievements so far in this respect?

- What have you done in a similar situation in the past that has worked for you?

- Are there any obstacles that you need to overcome? How do you think you might do this?

Options

This is a really exciting stage where the coachee is encouraged to think of all the possible ways in which they can move towards their goal. In many ways it can also be the most challenging. It involves brainstorming, which is not pinning the coachee down to actually taking any action but simply asking them to identify as many different possibilities as they can. Useful questions for the options stage include:

- What could you do as the next step (or perhaps the first step) towards reaching your goal?

- What else could you do? And what else? (Keep repeating this!)

- If time was not a factor, what could you do?

- What are the different ways in which you could approach this challenge?

- If you were someone else giving yourself advice, what would you say?

Will

Now we come on to the stage where the coachee has to decide on the action(s) they are committing themselves to taking. To do this, they select from their options the ones that they will choose to work on first. Useful questions for the will stage include:

- Which of the options will you choose? (maybe several)

- How will that help you to achieve your goal?

- How would you score your own level of commitment to achieving this goal on a scale of 0 to 10 (0 being 'absolutely not committed!' and 10 being 'totally committed')?

- When precisely are you going to start and finish each action step?

- What support do you need and from whom?

These are just examples, and there are many more questions that we can ask in each stage of the GROW model.[10]

When I introduce the GROW model in coaching training sessions, with examples of questions like the ones above, some people can initially feel a little awkward about the process as, for them, it just doesn't seem to flow. Of course, in the spirit of growth mindsets this is good! It means that they are struggling and therefore learning and creating new neuronal connections. Once people overcome this hurdle and progressively start to use coaching on a more regular basis, any doubts they have tend to fade as they begin to understand the benefits that can come from the coaching process. But for some people this does take time.

The GROW model can be used in its entirety in a full coaching session, or in the classroom it might be that only one of the four stages is focused on at a particular time. The way the questions are phrased above are in adult language and may need to be modified for younger students. Coaching used with a student can move

---

10 There are some free downloadable coaching resources at: http://tonyswainston.com/ free-resources/.

What mindsets are all about

	Can the student ...	Examples of this:	
Creating	... create something new or develop an innovative point of view?	create, design, develop, formulate, write, assemble, construct	High cognitive demand
Evaluating	... give a judgement?	appraise, argue, defend, judge, select, support, value, evaluate	
Analysing	... distinguish between different parts?	appraise, compare, contrast, criticise, examine, experiment, question, test	
Applying	... use the information once shown how?	employ, illustrate, operate	
Understanding	... explain ideas or concepts?	classify, describe, discuss, explain, report, select, translate, paraphrase	
Remembering	... recall or remember the information?	define, duplicate, list, memorise, recall, repeat	Low cognitive demand

from reproducing to reasoning

them from simply receiving and repeating information to deeper reasoning that links with higher level learning. This can be viewed as moving the student from the lower to higher levels of Bloom's taxonomy. An updated and modern version of Bloom's taxonomy is shown below. Coaching can help you to help the students to move up to higher levels of cognitive demand.

Coaching also helps students to believe in their potential. As they begin to realise that solutions lie within themselves, so their confidence to take on more challenging situations will grow. This is all part of the development of a growth mindset.

More benefits of coaching

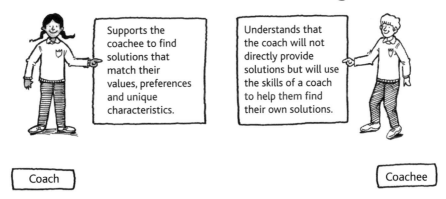

Supports the coachee to find solutions that match their values, preferences and unique characteristics.

Understands that the coach will not directly provide solutions but will use the skills of a coach to help them find their own solutions.

Coach

Coachee

Another great benefit of coaching is that it gives you the opportunity to build great relationships with both students and colleagues in your school. The more they are aware that you understand them, the more they will respond positively to you, and this will support the development of a mindset for success involving growth mindsets. In addition, and in terms of using coaching to support your leadership skills as a way of embedding a culture of mindset for success in your school, it is worth reflecting on the research carried out by Daniel Goleman which found that the most effective leaders use six styles at different times and to different degrees.[11]

----

11 See D. Goleman, R. Boyatzis and A. McKee, *Primal Leadership: Unleashing the Power of Emotional Intelligence* (Boston, MA: Harvard Business School Press, 2002), p. 55.

He says that these leadership styles can be learned and each of them has a link with EI.

1. Coercive: This leader gives out orders. Sometimes it has to be done!

2. Visionary: This leader has a powerful ability to articulate a vision and encourage people to follow them.

3. Affiliative: This leader likes to establish positive relationships by getting to know others.

4. Democratic: This leader focuses on decision making by winning consensus.

5. Pacesetting: This leader sets high performance standards for everyone, including her/himself. She/he walks the talk.

6. Coaching: This leader focuses on developing people. She/he is able to recognise hidden potential in individuals and how best to develop it.

Visionary leadership and coaching leadership both tend to facilitate long-term growth in a school. The leadership style that is probably least used is coaching, generally because of the time factor that was mentioned earlier on. When we are under pressure, and schools are often under pressure to perform, it may seem far quicker and easier to tell people what to do, rather than talk to them so they can find the best solution for themselves. Of course, this is the same in lessons taking place in classrooms. However, if schools are really to develop the potential within each individual, all staff and all pupils, then coaching is the way forward. And through coaching we will also be developing growth mindsets and a culture which embraces a mindset for success.

Coaching skills

A coach has three fundamental skills: listening, asking questions and reflecting back what the other person has said. These may seem to be very simple, but both reflective and deliberate practice must be used in order to constantly raise these skill levels.

Using our heads

1. Listening

As a coach I listen to the person as if they are a fascinating stranger (even if I 'know them' well).

I keep focused on them.

I listen for nuances in what they say.

I use my intuition.

I listen to what is being said beneath the words.

I listen for the content and also the intent and feeling in the message.

2. Asking questions

My questions always support the person I am coaching to find their own answers.

Effective questions help me connect with people in a more meaningful way.

I use questions to help me more fully understand the coachee's issue.

I employ a variety of questions including open ended, commitment, leading and reframing questions at times.

3. Reflecting back to the other person what they have said

This allows the coachee the space to reflect on what they have said so far – they may change their mind after hearing back what they have said.

I reflect back the words, thoughts and feelings that I have picked up from the coachee.

I try to use the same words that the coachee has used when reflecting back to them.

I have trained hundreds of people from schools around the world in the art and science of coaching. To begin with many people wonder what is different about coaching from what they already do, and to be frank what the big deal is all about. However, once they have spent time practising coaching with each other, and with people back in their schools, many tell me how it has impacted enormously on their effectiveness as teachers or as support staff.

Listening

Let's first of all consider listening. Are you a good listener? Are the people you know good listeners? If you have answered yes to both of these you will probably have great relationships with these people. Most of us are not as good at listening to others as we would like to be though, and also find it difficult to find other people who will really listen to us.

The Chinese symbol for listening gives a real sense of what true listening involves.

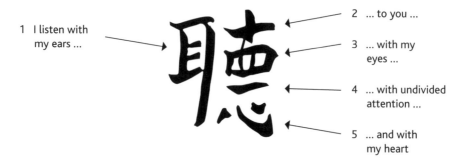

1 I listen with my ears ...

2 ... to you ...

3 ... with my eyes ...

4 ... with undivided attention ...

5 ... and with my heart

This is so powerful. Wouldn't it be wonderful if this kind of listening took place more often in all of our relationships and in all lessons? Many teachers and support staff that I have trained have decided to display this image of the elements of good listening in their classrooms as a reminder for both themselves and the students.

Questioning

In terms of questioning we can use these 'famous five' questions to great effect:

You might ask, 'Why should I not use "why"?' Well, the answer is that it can seem very accusatory for the person being asked the question, making them feel they need to justify their actions and potentially even inciting them to tell lies. (You might think here about the responses you may have had when asking a student, 'Why are you late to my lesson?')

Reflecting back

For reflecting back you can use sentence starters like the following:

> If I am understanding you correctly, what you are saying is ...
>
> Can I just clarify then: what happened was ...
>
> So at this stage you have said ...

Different schools invariably decide to journey along the path of coaching to varying degrees. As a leader in the school, whether it be in your own classroom or in a broader leadership role, coaching is a great tool. As a developmental tool, a coaching approach can add great value in classrooms and schools on its own. When it is focused on developing a mindset for success in a school, the resultant synergy is very powerful.[12]

In Part III, we will be looking at the challenge of developing a mindset for success in schools. Change is always difficult, particularly when it involves deeply held beliefs, attitudes, expectations and habits. For growth mindsets to become part of the culture of the school there will need to be a focus on various groups of people: teachers, support staff, parents, governors and, of course, the students will all benefit from mindset training. The aim of the training is to develop a common language around growth mindsets which everybody can contribute to and benefit from.

We will discover how we can successfully manage and lead a change of mindset throughout the whole school community. We will see how working on aspects of motivation and EI will help us to bring about the sustainable change we desire, and how this will help those students who are stuck in the valley of poverty of aspirations to climb out and fulfil their potential. The TEA-R model will also be introduced as a way of explaining to students how they can take more control of their thoughts and emotions. In addition, the benefits of action research on mindsets will be covered. Finally, we will look at the kind of mindset for success plan that you may decide is most appropriate for you to adopt in your school over a 12 month period.

---

12 See my book *Coaching for Change: Creating a Self-Development Culture* (London: Optimus Education, 2012) for a programme of twilight sessions which schools can use to train staff in coaching.

Part III

How to change the mindsets of a school community

Chapter 6
It's about a culture change

Establishing a culture of possibilities

I presume by this stage that you have decided to bring about a mindset change in your school. It could be that you are the head teacher and therefore looking at the big picture or you may be a teacher wanting to bring about change in your own classroom. Some people may ask why it's important to change anything if it is all going fairly well or even very well. The answer is that we really have little option in education if we want to advance and move forward. Things change every day and we live with the paradox that change is the only constant. How we adapt to the changing circumstances around us is what will determine our success. But it is far more important than this, of course.

We want to constantly improve what we presently do in schools because everything we do impacts on the present and future happiness and success of the children who come into our care. And part of looking to constantly change, and creating a culture of change, is that we are then modelling to the pupils that we are prepared to adapt what we do – with the inherent risk of sometimes getting it wrong. And along the journey we are learning and therefore benefiting from our mistakes. As we will see, this is the key characteristic of a growth mindset. But it is also true that by creating a culture of change in our classrooms and schools we are also opening up a culture of possibilities. We want children to feel the excitement of growth, which is a very natural feature of their lives and all our lives, but which can, if we are not careful, be educated out of them.

We know that change can be extremely difficult. We all want, to a greater or lesser extent, to stay in our known comfort zones. These are the places where we know how things operate, where we can play out our daily roles without too much effort or discomfort. Furthermore, the evidence suggests that most change initiatives in organisations fail. Therefore it's important that we have a clear vision of where we want to get to and why we want to get there. (In Appendix A you will find the school focus and goal setting document that I give to schools when they are embarking on a mindset for success programme with me.) Critical in all of this is the buy-in from the senior leadership team (SLT). If you are the head teacher or principal then your enthusiasm for the project will be the greatest factor in its success. If you are a teacher in the school then you need to be sure that the head teacher and the SLT are fully supportive of your work. I am sure that with determination you will still do great things in your own classroom, but if you are looking to establish a common language of growth and development for all individuals then you will need support from those who make the decisions.

Have you ever wondered what is meant by a culture? Walk into any classroom in any school and you will be instantly immersed in a sensory avalanche that provides you with your own personal understanding about the way things operate in this environment. We loosely call this a culture. Some people define a culture as 'the way we do things around here', and some add to this that the true culture is best observed when the boss isn't around. The complex thing about a culture is that it is made up of so many components that it may at times seem almost impossible to know where to start if we want to change it.

In broad terms we can think of an organisational culture as made up of three distinct entities. (In a school what I am referring to here as the organisation may be a classroom, a department, the staffroom, the office, the student body or a variety of other subdivisions within the school, as well as the whole school. As individuals we also bring our own personal culture into the mix. Each element impacts upon the whole culture.) These three entities are the way things are structured, the signs and symbols we see around the school, and the values of people that in turn drive their behaviour.

Focusing on the culture within a classroom, the structures include things like the way the teacher divides up the lessons, bells, seating plans and where books and other resources are stored. The signs and symbols include things like displays on the walls, the school uniform and the way the teacher is dressed. Certain micro-behaviours are also evident and these include the way the children talk to each other, the way the children and adults interact with each other and talk to the teacher and other adults, and the level of accepted noise in the classroom at different times. However, it is the underlying values, which drive these behaviours, that really have the greatest impact on the culture. These values permeate the environment and create a belief, or otherwise, in people that there is an authentic focus on achievement for every individual (in its broadest sense of both academic and social success), a desire to help each other, a sense of wanting to get to know each other, a feeling of being fulfilled by the learning taking place (which may be referred to as an example of self-actualisation), an understanding that failure enables us to learn, a sense of safety in taking risks, a sincere level of respect and an emphasis on resilience.

My strong belief, based on my experience of working with schools, is that the culture – determined overwhelmingly by the values that drive the behaviours – can be significantly and positively influenced by a determined focus on the principles of a growth mindset.

Are we doing the right thing in our schools?

There is an old saying that 'if we keep on doing what we've always done, we will keep on getting what we've always had'. The bad news is that this is completely wrong. If we keep on doing the same things (even if we put more and more effort into them) then we will be on a road to failure. The only certainty in the world, the only constant, is change. This ensures that many things which work and are relevant today may not work and may not be relevant tomorrow. Stephen Covey said, 'Management is efficiency in climbing the ladder of success; leadership determines whether the ladder is leaning against the right wall,'[1] and as leaders in our schools and in our classrooms, we really do need to know that we are putting the ladder up against the right wall. At the same time, we also have to constantly check to make sure that what may have been the right wall to climb yesterday is still the best wall to climb today.

....

1 S. Covey, *The Seven Habits of Highly Effective People: Restoring the Character Ethic* (New York: Free Press, 1989), p. 101.

This book is about change and change is happening all the time in schools, but we need to ask whether the changes are always leading to greater levels of happiness and achievement for our children. At the moment, schools in the UK are being 'encouraged' to become academies. Yet the jury is still out on whether academies actually raise standards in our schools. Alongside this is the question of whether the standards that we are at present measuring are the right ones. But everyone agrees that things do need to change. We can't hang on forever to an education system that has been driven by an industrial model of conformity, uniformity and quality control. The world is crying out for individuality and fresh, new solutions to ongoing problems. As Einstein is reported to have said: 'We can't solve problems by using the same kind of thinking we used when we created them.' We owe it to our students, communities and the whole world to find an education system which best fits the needs of the present day. In my view, this is where Carol Dweck and her wonderful work on mindsets can help us to develop an approach to education which encourages every individual to fulfil their own potential.

The adoption of a mindset for success culture in schools will inevitably require change, and change is not easy because, as we have seen, many of us prefer to stay with the familiar even if it is not necessarily producing the results we want. This is true in schools and in our lives in general. An integral part of a culture which has a mindset for success is that change is happening on a regular basis, but it is important for us to manage it in schools otherwise people can be overwhelmed by its apparently relentless nature. It is therefore worthwhile looking at how change takes place and how it impacts on our level of success.

Charles Handy, as part of his work on organisational behaviour and management, represents the change that takes place in an organisation like a school as a sigmoid curve (a bit like a letter 'S' on its side).[2] The sigmoid curve illustrates the pathway of every successful action carried out by human beings. The following is my adaptation of the Handy model and can help us to reflect on how we might implement a mindset for success in our school in a way that allows for progressively increasing levels of success.

....

2   See CareerTech Testing Center, The sigmoid curve, personal learning, and the 'business' of education (30 November 2010). Available at: http://careertechtesting.blogspot.co.uk/2010/11/sigmoid-curve-personal-learning-and.html.

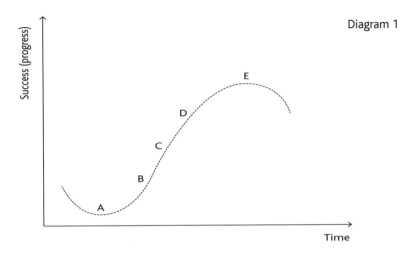

Diagram 1 shows how whenever we try something new – for example, bringing ideas about mindsets into our school – there is a dip (A) in the level of success we previously experienced. This is due to various factors, such as the new learning, time and money we have to invest in the project. However, eventually we start to reap the benefits of the new activity and progress to an upward curve of success (B, C and D). Then the increased benefits start to tail off and plateau (E). As time goes by we start to experience a fall in our success level from this activity. The key question is, where on the curve do you think it is best to bring in a new activity? Would it be at A, B, C, D or E?

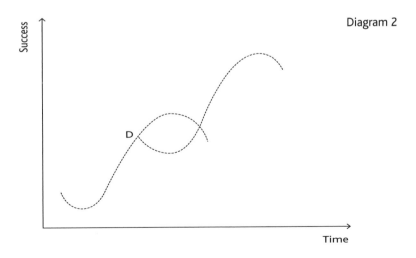

It is hard to be precise about this, and of course this is only a model, but it is a model that nevertheless seems to replicate the way that our level of success in carrying out any activity will change over time. Handy suggests that around D (as shown in diagram 2) is the best time to change. How do we know when we have reached D? Well, the answer is that we will not know with certainty. We have to use our instincts on this, and perhaps sense the 'thin slice' of what is happening both inside the organisation as well as in the wider world. We also need to be constantly on the lookout for new ideas and new methods of doing what we do.

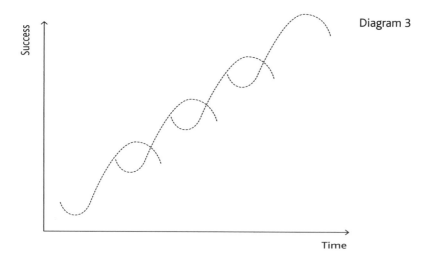

Diagram 3

Diagram 3 shows how with constant change at the right time we can experience an upward trend in our level of success. This links with the notion of deliberate practice. It also illustrates how any mindset intervention is not a one-off activity but has to be an ongoing process that builds up step by step.

Here are a few questions you might ask yourself about the curve of change, with some suggested answers.

1.   Why don't I look to change something at A, B, C or E?

  ● Changing at A would not have allowed you to reap any benefits from the change you have brought in before trying something new. You are still in the trough of lowering your success level from what it was before. Another change will potentially lower your success level still further. This could lead to you feeling overwhelmed and dispirited. This can happen when too much change is going on at too rapid a pace in a classroom (or school). The students would also likely feel overwhelmed.

- Changing at B is a bit like changing at A. It is still happening too quickly.

- Changing at C would probably be okay, as you have given the new action time to really have an impact. However, you might wish to allow this to go a bit further still to D.

- Changing at E on the face of it seems sensible. However, you will now be feeling that it is becoming a struggle to keep things improving, so you will be feeling a pressure to try something new. This is not a good state in which to be. You will feel anxiety and when this happens your higher level thought processes will be hijacked by your survival instincts.[3] The job of the amygdala in your brain is to raise the alarm when you are threatened. Now emotions in your body take over and you are in the classic fight, flight or freeze state. Your thinking brain is disabled and you cannot think clearly or rationally. In addition your concentration levels and memory ability are also reduced.

2. When I change something do I have to leave the old thing behind?

   No. You don't have to throw the baby out with the bathwater, although in the long term you may find that your baby has now grown and you need to allow it to move on.

3. What is the time lag involved before I get to D?

   This is impossible to say. It could be days, weeks or even years. This is why we need to be constantly alert to changes taking place.

---

3 'Emotional hijacking' is a term used by Daniel Goleman in his book *Emotional Intelligence: Why It Can Matter More Than IQ* (New York: Bantam Books, 2006).

4. How does this relate to me in the classroom aspiring to be a highly effective teacher and incorporating mindsets ideas into my lessons?

    We need to be on the lookout for new methods of providing excellent learning opportunities for the students, and building a mindset for success will support this enormously. If we just keep doing the same things without modifying these or looking at new ideas then our effectiveness will decline. (Even in a marriage or relationship we have to consider changing things as time moves on. Our children grow and move on, we grow and therefore change as individuals, and many other circumstances around us are constantly shifting. Without looking to introduce new ways of doing things together we may find that our marriage or relationship starts to deteriorate.)

I believe that the key message from Handy's model is that effective change towards a mindset for success requires a thoroughly thought-through process which involves a progressive drip-feed approach, with each element building on the previous success. My hope is that this book will provide you with the clarity about how you can implement a mindset for success culture in your school in an efficient, effective and sustainable way.

The biggest challenge that we need to overcome, if we are to bring about a mindset for success culture, involves encouraging as many individuals as possible to adapt or change some of their beliefs. Ultimately, we are working to provide the very best chances in life for the pupils that we teach and it is their mindsets on which we are most focused. The more they have a growth mindset, the more they will be able to tackle daily challenges with confidence, optimism and success. However, we will only be successful in developing constructive growth mindsets in students if a significant number of the adults they interact with also have growth mindsets, and therefore deliver positive messages to the students both in school and at home. In the next chapter, therefore, we will be looking at how we go about changing the mindsets of individuals and groups of people in, and associated with, the school.

Chapter 7
Changing the minds of individuals

Changing the minds of teachers

If you were asked to describe the difference between the mind and the brain, what would you say? In Chapter 5 we described the brain as the physical entity in our heads and the mind as the outcome of the way our brains function. You will recall that an exciting development over the past few years has been our understanding of the brain's plasticity and that it can, to a certain extent, change its physical structure through the way we think or the way that our mind operates. It is important for us to remember that the way we think with our minds is a result of the data we have stored in our brains, and this data comprises not only the knowledge and information we have acquired but also all of our habits, attitudes, expectations, beliefs and values.

All of these associations are created by connections in our brain (neurons connecting with other neurons) which are pretty much hardwired. This may lead to the idea that changing our minds (by changing our brains) is not going to be possible. Well, the bad news is that it's not easy, but the good news is that it is possible. The way our brains have become hardwired with neuronal connections allows us to carry out most of the things we do on a daily basis without consciously thinking about them. Once you learn to walk, talk, tie your shoelaces, ride a bike and drive a car then most of the complex actions involved in each of these activities happen without us having to consciously think. This frees up our conscious mind for the tasks that absolutely require this. So, our subconscious (or unconscious) mind carries out most of our actions and the conscious mind is used to fine tune the detail of what we do.

There are different models that try to describe this process. Daniel Kahneman refers to fast and slow thinking.[1] The fast thinking comes from our subconscious mind and the slow thinking comes from our conscious mind. The reason why all of this is important is that changing our minds requires, to some degree, a rewiring. And the problem with this is that it's not easy to remove wiring in our brains without some sort of physical intervention, and clearly this is not entirely desirable! However, we can add new wiring, which we are doing all the time as we think. To change our minds (or, in other words, to change a belief, habit, attitude or expectation), we can start to add wiring that counterbalances what already exists. Take a fixed mindset belief that someone might have about intelligence, which is that individual intelligence is set and there is not much we can do to change it. If this is a deep-seated belief then it's not likely that it will change overnight. On top of this there can be a reluctance to give up a belief that we have formed, because we tend to think that this belief is part of who we are. And just as we would be clearly reluctant to lose an arm or another part of our body, we can also feel a sense of loss when giving up a belief we have. Changing our belief about Santa Claus may be an example for many of us of the loss we felt when we altered a belief.

This gives us some clue as to why it can be difficult to change the minds of teachers once they have adopted a belief. And because teachers have such powerful beliefs, which are so deeply felt that they tend to guide and drive their actions on a daily basis, it is not easy for them to change their minds or change their beliefs. How then is this achieved? Well, in most cases, I would say that this needs to happen in a fairly steady way as part of a gradual process. My experience of working on shifting mindsets in schools is that just when you think you have made progress, something is said that seems to torpedo this idea.

An example of this occurred in one school where I was doing mindset training. After having worked with the school staff more than half a dozen times, one member of support staff observed that the school could use the new knowledge of mindsets with groups of HAPs (high achieving pupils), MAPs (middle achieving pupils) and LAPs (low achieving pupils). The challenge here was how something that was accepted in the culture of the school as a useful way of describing and differentiating between pupils may have unintended negative consequences in terms

---

1   D. Kahneman, *Thinking, Fast and Slow* (London: Penguin, 2012).

of any attempt to develop growth mindsets. The positive outcome from the resulting discussion was that the potential hidden messages behind HAPs, MAPs and LAPs labelling was brought out into the open and discussed in a conscious way, so that the teachers and support staff were more aware of possible dangers from labels that we attach to individuals or groups of students.

It's important to provide teachers with evidence about IQ measures and the way that mindsets impact on the learning and development of children, and indeed all of us. A starting point in terms of IQ intelligence (a measure of short-term memory, analytical thinking, mathematical ability and spatial recognition) is to make it clear that this is not fixed. This is something which, maybe surprisingly, is not well known by many people in education.

But just giving this information to teachers may not be enough to change their belief about IQ; rather it requires a drip-feed approach. A one-off twilight session for teachers on mindset may be interesting and might even have an immediate impact on some classroom and whole-school practice. However, it is very unlikely to have longevity as teachers may well revert back to their default mode of (subconscious) thinking once the overwhelming complexity of the school environment begins to overtake their conscious attempt to employ mindset thinking in their classroom. Teachers need to commit themselves to deliberate practice, and this is more likely to happen through a series of training inputs over a period of time. I would recommend that at least a 12 month period will be required for a mindset for success culture to be established, with further ongoing checks to ensure the culture of growth mindsets remains embedded in the school.

Changing the minds of support staff

Many of the techniques applied to supporting the change of teachers' mindsets apply equally to everyone else in the school. The drip-feed message must also go into changing the mindsets of support staff, including classroom support assistants, office staff and other members of the support staff including caretakers and lunchtime supervisors. Any parents involved in voluntary work in the school should also be included. The point is that if we are to bring about a culture change in the school it has to involve all members. During my own work in schools on culture change, I have found it fascinating to witness how different groups can interpret the culture of the school in very different ways. The important point to remember about culture is that perception rules. It doesn't matter what the actual culture of the school is like, because it is the perception that will determine how people behave. If individuals feel disenfranchised from the core purpose of the school they will act accordingly and not feel fully motivated and committed. Consequently we must involve all support staff, because it is both morally right to do so and without their commitment we will not achieve as great a success.

One of the ways we can try to get commitment is to involve support staff in the same training as teachers. This can happen in a number of ways. Because of the logistics of taking people off timetable during the school day, the head teacher may decide to release support staff from their normal duties during the school day for mindset training, then the teachers receive the same training at the end of the school day. In this way, support staff feel they are an integral part of the mindset initiative and vision.

An interesting story about how the vision of an organisation can powerfully influence how people work dates back to when the Americans were trying to get a man on the moon. In the mid-1960s, so the story goes, John F. Kennedy was visiting the NASA space centre at Cape Canaveral. As he was taken on a guided tour around the complex he took the time to ask a number of employees about their work. This included three men who were in overalls and carrying out various manual tasks. When he asked the first of these men, 'What do you do here?' the man replied, 'I'm earning a living.' Kennedy smiled and moved on to meet the second of the men and asked him the same question. This man replied, 'I empty the bins and clean away the rubbish.' Kennedy smiled again and moved on until he met the third man who was sweeping the floor. Again, he asked the same question, and probably expected a very obvious answer. But this time an enormous smile appeared on the man's face and he replied, 'Mr President, I'm helping to put a man on the moon.'

This incident may never have actually happened, but it illustrates beautifully how our attitude to any given task can be radically altered by how we see that it fits into a higher purpose or vision that we believe in. The higher purpose of mindsets might be expressed as providing the young people in our schools with the opportunity to take on challenges with confidence in order to fulfil their immense potential in a multitude of ways. You may, of course, express the purpose of mindsets within your school in many different ways. The important thing is to get all members of the school to believe in the importance of the mindset for success initiative, and this is more likely to be achieved if everyone is fully informed about mindsets and involved in the training.

One way of enabling support staff to feel cared for and valued is for them to work on a small mindset project together. This might be formally termed as action research (for more on this see Chapter 9) or more informally it might be thought of as testing out an idea. It could be something like, 'The way in which words we use as educators can be used to develop a growth mindset' or 'Techniques used to change the mindsets of a group of children who display poor behaviour'. The level at which we can get support staff to feel valued and involved in the mindset initiative will significantly impact on the development of a constructive culture with a mindset for success.

Changing the minds of pupils – breaking the cycle

It is ultimately the pupils that we are working for, and even at a very early age, they will have started to form very strong opinions and beliefs. There are some key influences on the way their minds will have developed, including the family, peers, the media and indeed the school. All of this may seem to make our task, as educators, of changing their mindsets somewhat impossible. But it isn't. Teachers make a real difference to the development of the pupils in their care (though it is important for us to be honest and say that some teachers make a much bigger difference than others, and that some may unfortunately even inhibit the learning of the students). All the research tells us that this is the case. The combined impact of all the teachers and support staff in the school can be enormous. It is crucial, therefore, that a consistent message is delivered to the pupils, and this is why any mindset intervention should involve everyone in a holistic approach. The consistent and constant message they receive then comes from the culture of possibilities in the school.

TEA-R

All adults in the school need to be aware that, for many students, a powerful, negatively self-fulfilling cycle will need to be broken. I call this the TEA-R cycle: *thoughts* impact on our *emotions* which then impact on our *actions* which bring about the *results* we get. And so the cycle continues, with the results feeding back into our thought process and beginning the cycle once more. If we want to get different results then we need a new TEA-R cycle. But where do we tear, or break into, the TEA-R cycle?

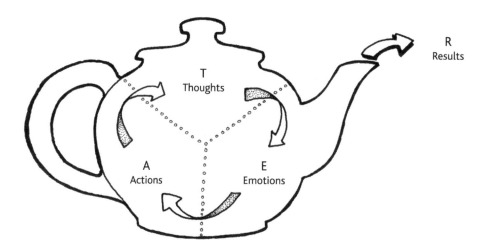

As educators we may at times focus on the actions of an individual and try to persuade them to change these. However, this is often working backwards, and it can be hard for children to change their actions when their thoughts and emotions are driving them along a particular route that is well established. A more powerful way is to get them to consider their thoughts and how these are either helping them or hindering their progress. (It should be noted that it may, on occasion, be possible to persuade a child to change their actions which can break the cycle. However, if the deep-seated thoughts are still functioning in an old TEA-R cycle then they might easily default back to this when they are not consciously 'thinking'.)

In describing to pupils how the TEA-R cycle works, you can use a glass cup or teapot so they can see what is inside. You then take a teabag with string attached to it and put it into the pot and pour cold water onto it. If you leave it undisturbed for a minute or so the water will not colour very much. Even if you dunk the teabag up and down a few times the water may not change colour a great deal. Then pour out the water and remove the teabag. Take another teabag, put it into the empty teapot and this time pour boiling water onto it. After a few seconds the water should start to colour around the teabag. And if you dunk the teabag up and down in the hot water, this time the water will get progressively darker. Continue to do this for a little while, letting the teabag stew in the water, and you will, of course, find that the water gets very dark. You might then empty out the water and teabag from the pot once more and use another teabag of a different flavour (coloured fruit teas work well), repeating the process just described, first with cold water and then with hot water.

The different teabags represent different thoughts, the temperature of the water represents the level of emotion associated with our thoughts, and the number of times we dunk the teabag into the water represents the number of times we repeat our thoughts. The degree to which the water is coloured represents the level of impact the thoughts have had on us and our minds. Our mind can get into a very dark place with unhelpful thoughts. We often refer to 'stewing in our thoughts' in the same way as we refer to tea being stewed when left for a long time in a teapot.

The point of this extended metaphor is that we want to give the pupils a way to understand that they can change their thoughts and that they can have control over this if they choose to do so. This may be one of the most important messages we can give to them. This is part of pupils learning about metacognition, or thinking about their thinking, which will support them throughout their lives. It is fun and powerful. Once again, it is important that when we work with pupils on mindsets we recognise that it always works best if it is a drip-feed process rather than a one-off message. The model given here is a useful way of giving the students a tool to use to think about their thinking. However, it works best when we frequently refer back to this and remind them that they do have the ability to control their thoughts.

In this book we will look at a number of ways in which we can support children to develop a constructive growth mindset. Equally, however, with the wrong kind of message (which we can sometimes give with the best of intentions, according to the law of unintended consequences) we can push them into destructive fixed mindsets. (Praise is an example of how the things we often intend to be highly positive can have some negative unanticipated consequences.) Many of the teachers that I've been working with on the mindset for success programme are dealing with very powerful negative self-fulfilling TEA-R cycles in many pupils. These have been hardwired into their brains – for example, sometimes three or four generations of their families have been living on benefits. Children in these circumstances clearly face a difficult and perilous climb if they are to get out of the pit of low aspirations, often created by negative family talk and reinforced by unhelpful self-talk. Many children have to battle with what I call 'the valley of the poverty of aspirations'. We need to support them in their struggle to climb out of this valley in order that they can operate on a relatively level playing field with other children.

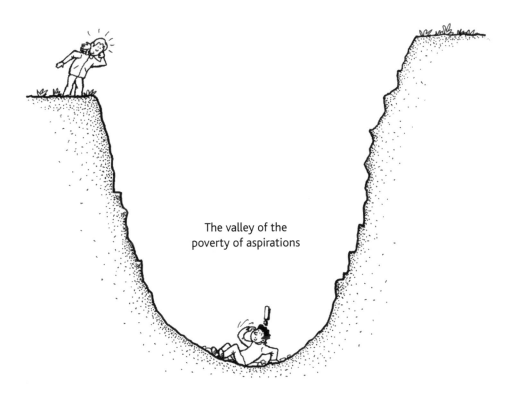

The valley of the
poverty of aspirations

A note on metacognition: meta strictly speaking means 'beyond' and cognition is how we go about acquiring knowledge and understanding through our thoughts, experience and senses. Putting the two together gives us metacognition, which effectively takes us beyond the first stage of acquiring knowledge and understanding to the higher level of 'cognition about cognition', 'thinking about thinking' or 'knowing about knowing'. In terms of its use with mindsets, metacognition helps the students to understand how they can take charge of their beliefs, habits and attitudes towards learning so that they can learn more effectively. From the TEA-R model, we can see how our emotions are influenced by our thoughts and how our emotions guide the approach (actions) we take. In this case, metacognition is about the way in which the students think about the way they are thinking in order to then think more constructively and in such a way that it positively influences their emotions, actions and results.

Changing the minds of parents

Like me, you may have come across teachers who believe that the impact of the home is so strong that it is almost pointless for a school to try to do anything to change the beliefs of students. Although nobody would deny the powerful, and sometimes unintentionally negative, influence that parents have on their children's beliefs, schools can do a lot to counterbalance this by encouraging more constructive beliefs in students. But if a teacher believes that this is impossible then this will be true for them. Just like the children, these teachers will create a truth around them that provides evidence for their belief. It is not necessarily done for any negative reason, but rather because we all want to live in a world where our inner beliefs are supported by the world we see and experience around us, even if our beliefs are not necessarily supportive of us in a healthy way. The reason for this is that the alternative would be to live in a world where what we experience contradicts our beliefs, and the result of this is that we would then feel we are crazy. However, if we change our beliefs then what we experience in the world around us will be very different. Sun Tzu summed this up when he said 'Change the way you look at things and the things you look at change.'[2]

One of the challenges we have in engaging parents is that the parents of the children we most wish to see are often the ones least likely to come into the school. I have heard these referred to as 'Heineken' parents (named after the 1970s Heineken TV commercial which used the slogan 'Heineken refreshes the parts other beers cannot reach'), because they are reached only by some schools that other schools fail to reach! There can be a range of reasons for this, including parents having had a negative experience of schooling themselves and therefore not wanting to come into the school, parents who don't want to come in to hear what they think will be unfavourable comments about their child, and parents who frankly don't value education. They may even fear the idea of stepping into a school building.

However, to have the best chance of success it's important to involve as many parents as possible in the mindset for success programme. They can add so much weight to the messages we want to give to their children, so involving them in the

2   Quoted in M. Michalko, *Thinkertoys: A Handbook of Creative-Thinking Techniques* (Berkeley, CA: Ten Speed Press, 2006), p. 374.

strategy is crucial. However, the idea of coming into school to listen to a so-called expert, like myself, talking to them about this thing called 'mindsets' may not seem very appealing for many busy parents. They might not understand what it is all about, and they might interpret the invitation to come into the school as something that is punitive rather than supportive. One strategy that some schools use is to involve the pupils in the evening or day event. In this way, the children can tell the story of mindsets powerfully in their own way to get the message across to their own parents as well as others. It can considerably support their understanding about mindsets as well.

It might be argued that it is part of human nature that we do things because we see some advantage to ourselves. We call this the WIIFM (what's in it for me) phenomenon. If we want to work with parents, we need to think about it from their point of view and their own WIIFM. The vast majority of parents want the very best for their children, but they may not view the 'very best for their children' in the same way that we do as educators.

It has been shown from research that parents' views about failure can significantly impact on the way their children approach challenges, and it appears that this might have a far stronger impact on the mindset of their children than the view that they might have about intelligence being fixed or developmental.[3] Therefore, this is one of the most important things to include in mindset training sessions for parents. A questionnaire to elicit their views about failure can be used as a starting point for discussion with parents about the importance of encouraging their children to take on tasks which at times they may not complete successfully, but at the same time may learn a tremendous amount from their failures. As with the pupils, it is important for us to maintain a positive and constructive growth mindset about the potential of parents to themselves alter some of their beliefs and the language they use with their children. Many parents will simply not have had the opportunity to consider the impact that their own beliefs and language have on their children. The information on mindsets and the mindset tools that we can provide them with may therefore act like a springboard for them to explore further and then notice the benefits that come to their children.

....

3   See K. Haimovitz and C. Dweck, What predicts children's fixed and growth intelligence mind-sets? Not their parents' views of intelligence but their parents' views of failure, *Psychological Science*, 27(6) (2016), 859–869.

Involving governors

The governors of the school are influential in the way that the school develops its culture, and they can bring an external point of view which supports the development of constructive growth mindsets. They also support the vision and direction of the school, and as such they are very important members of the school community. Governors will, of course, need to be made aware of what the key messages are behind the notion of growth and fixed mindsets. My experience in running training in schools is that the best way governors can embrace these ideas is by attending the training sessions offered to teachers and support staff. I also welcome their presence at the parents' evening sessions and assemblies provided for the children. In this way they are able to witness first-hand the kinds of questions that people might ask, the way that staff and pupils are engaging with the initiative, and the impact that the training is having on the culture of the school. Governors will also come from a variety of different work and professional backgrounds where they have their own valuable stories to tell about the influence that mindsets can have on the effectiveness of individuals in an organisation and on the culture of the organisation. Governors complete the circle of all elements in the school being involved in the initiative.

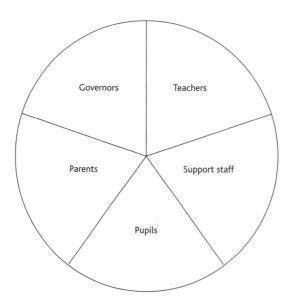

In the next chapter we will look at some other factors to take into consideration as we build a mindset for success in a school. These include the part played by EI and how this links with growth mindsets, overcoming the cynics that we may encounter on our journey, and how we can enable the mindset success culture to be sustained. In addition, we will look at the way that the words we use can powerfully support the development of growth mindsets, the importance of motivation in all we do and, finally, a plan for a 12 month programme of mindset development for schools.

Chapter 8
Further elements that support success

It's all about EI

Successful implementation of a constructive mindset culture in your school will most likely happen if it is part of a general way of thinking that values EI as much as IQ. Daniel Goleman's famous book, *Emotional Intelligence: Why it Can Matter More Than IQ*, brought to the attention of the general public, leaders and teachers the importance of EI in our personal and work lives.

There are different models of EI but they all embrace somewhat similar aspects of how we operate as human beings. The model below, which I use with schools, is adapted from Goleman. It has five dimensions, and it is the first of these that is most important – knowing myself or *self-awareness*. In many ways this is the foundation of all the other elements. Lao-Tzŭ said, 'He who knows others is clever, but he who knows himself is enlightened.'[1]

---

1   L. Cranmer-Byng and S. A. Kapadi (eds), *The Sayings of Lao-Tzŭ*, tr. L. Giles (New York: E. P. Dutton, 1905), p. 44.

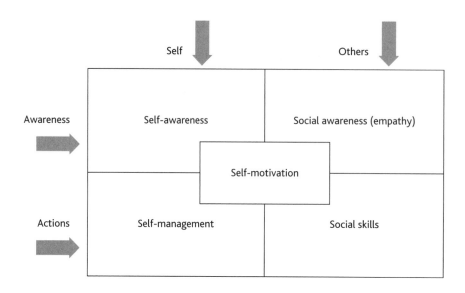

We can see in the matrix that after we understand ourselves we can move vertically or horizontally. Vertically we can move into the self-management dimension where we can take responsibility and control for the way that we operate, or horizontally we can move into the dimension of social awareness (or empathy) where the focus is on trying to understand other people. When we are able to manage ourselves and have empathy for other people, then we can move into the fourth dimension of social skills or being able to effectively manage and work with other people. You can see that self-motivation is also an integral part of the EI model shown here.

I am regularly asked during training sessions whether EI is something that people can develop. Research carried out by Goleman and others reveals that EI (and its associated measurement called EQ or emotional quotient) can be developed equally as much as IQ. I always say to people that, in my view, the biggest factor that determines an individual's ability to increase their EI is their desire to do so. I have met some people in schools and in business who are determined not to develop their EI because, quite frankly, they don't believe that it is important. They may consider that these 'soft skills' make no difference to the way an organisation operates and to the level of success that results. The research tells us something quite different.

I will now expand a little on the five aspects of EI which might help to support your understanding. As you read these definitions you might reflect on yourself and your own level of EI.

1. Self-awareness

Self-awareness is our ability to recognise how we are feeling, to understand how our emotions affect the way that we behave or act (once again you might reflect on this in terms of the TEA-R model discussed in Chapter 7) and to appreciate how we normally respond in a given situation. The more self-aware we are, the more we are in alignment with the way that other people see us. It is also a measure of our understanding of what we are presently good at and the things we need to improve on (in terms of the coaching GROW model, this is the R or current reality).

2. Self-management

When we manage our emotions we are able to stay focused, think clearly and behave appropriately in emotional situations. If we can't manage our emotions then we might find ourselves in situations where we behave in a rash way and then regret our actions later on.

3. Self-motivation

Self-motivation is our ability to be highly focused and committed to a goal, using our deepest emotions to support us on the journey. Our level of motivation links with our resilience, perseverance and grit which are all key aspects of a growth mindset. It enables us to deal with obstacles and setbacks in an effective way which is an essential characteristic of a growth mindset.

4. Social awareness/empathy

Empathy is our ability to understand a situation from another person's point of view; in this way we are able to respond far better to their emotions. Without self-awareness it is impossible to empathise with other people, because if we cannot understand our own emotions then we will struggle to understand the emotions of others.

5. Social skills

Our social skills determine our ability to manage, work with, inspire and influence other people on an emotional level. It is essential if we are to be able to work with others in teams and demonstrate effective leadership. Our social skills are therefore a foundation for the healthy relationships we will have with those around us.

You might like to look at the following 15 statements and decide how you would rate yourself on each of these. Use a scale as follows:

- 1 indicates that the statement does *not* apply at all to me.

- 3 indicates that the statement applies about *half* the time to me.

- 5 indicates that the statement *always* applies to me.

Further elements that support success

		Score from 1 to 5
1	I can usually recognise when I am stressed	
2	If I need to I can consciously alter my mood or my frame of mind	
3	I am able to prioritise things and focus on them	
4	I make a point of listening to and trying to understand other people	
5	When other people speak I show respect and I don't interrupt them	
6	If I lose my temper I'm aware of this immediately	
7	I don't allow difficult situations to get me down	
8	When I have difficult things to do I am able to keep motivated	
9	I always try to see things from another person's point of view	
10	I enjoy listening to others and I'm good at it	
11	I know what makes me happy	
12	I do not let stressful situations linger with me	
13	I'm very good at meeting deadlines	
14	I sense very well and can tell when somebody is not happy with me	
15	I enjoy, and I'm good at, adapting and mixing with lots of different people	

You can now record your scores for the statements in the grid below and then calculate a total for each of the five emotional competencies.

Self-awareness		Self-management		Self-motivation		Social awareness/ empathy		Social skills	
1		2		3		4		5	
6		7		8		9		10	
11		12		13		14		15	
Total		Total		Total		Total		Total	

Although this is only a very brief analysis, it will have given you a flavour of what the five EI competencies are about. There are a limited number of questions here so don't take it too seriously, but if you have a score between 10 and 15 for any of the competencies then you may consider this a strength, if you have a score between 5 and 9 then you might want to give this competency some attention, and if you have a score of 3 or 4 then you might want to give some real priority to developing this.

From this brief overview of EI, it is perhaps clear that students with high levels of EI are going to have a far better chance of being happy and successful in life, and this very much links with ideas around mindsets. We might refer to these qualities as life skills. In fact, Goleman's research has shown that the level of success of an individual will be determined more by their EQ than their IQ. IQ is the ticket that can get you off on a journey, but EQ is the richness of the journey you make. Other findings, including Hattie's meta-research, are revealing how developing the soft skills in pupils has a significant positive impact on their IQ scores and their learning in school. Some people may challenge the notion of EQ and even wonder whether it exists as something which can be accurately measured. It is worth mentioning here that IQ is also a murky concept with many definitions provided by a range of experts, but generally focusing on analytical reasoning, verbal skills, spatial ability, attention, memory and judgement. In any school, the higher the levels of EI, the greater will be the corresponding levels of human interaction with the inevitable footprint of success.

Overcoming the cynics and the tipping point

Inevitably, there will be some people who won't be totally convinced about the benefits of developing a growth mindset. They may have arguments which are very persuasive and it is only right that people should have the opportunity to express their views. In my opinion, it is important for us to ask ourselves these three questions when confronted by sceptics:

1. Are their views sincerely felt or are they trying to use this as a vehicle to express some other dissatisfaction that they are at present experiencing?

2. Are they likely to influence other people and turn them off developing a culture of constructive mindsets?

3. Can we win them around quickly or will it take time?

Our response to the cynics will depend on what our answers are to these three questions. For example, reflecting on the first of the questions, if we believe that they are expressing a sincere opinion then the best thing to do is to present the research evidence which supports the views that growth mindsets work and help to develop the child. You will find a number of examples in this book that you can use and, in general, this tends to convince most people. If, on the other hand, they are merely being argumentative or blocking, or they wish to express some sense of unhappiness about life in school (it can be a range of things), then it would be wise to find out what their motive is so that you can deal with it appropriately.

Adlerian psychology tells us that three As (attention seeking, aggression, avoidance of failure) and a P (power) describe the needs that people are trying to fulfil when they are reacting in an apparently confrontational and unhelpful way.[2] Both children and adults can have the same needs at times, so it might be useful to reflect on this when dealing with difficult adults in the school as well as pupils with behavioural problems. If we can understand the need they are trying to satisfy, in a manner that may not always be terribly constructive, then we will be in a far stronger position to deal with it appropriately.

....

2   T. Sweeney, *Adlerian Counseling* (1st edn) (Muncie, IN: Accelerated Development, 1989), p. 171.

You might want to think about a situation you have experienced when a teacher or member of support staff has raised objections to an idea, and you suspect the objectives are not sincerely felt but rather a smokescreen for something else. Do they simply want to be the centre of attention? Are they angry about something? Are they afraid that mindsets (in this case) might reveal a weakness in them that they would prefer to be hidden away? Do they want to exert power over you? Or is it more than one of these motives? If you can try to determine the real reason for their intransigence, then you will be in a far stronger position and have a very good chance of being able to tackle it sensitively.

For example, if we discover that the person is after attention, then we might try to involve them in giving presentations to other staff on how they have used mindsets in their own classroom. On the other hand, if we determine that it is avoidance of failure (a teacher who is afraid of taking on new ideas), then it may be more appropriate to find ways of lessening their anxiety. We may, for example, try to match certain key ideas in mindsets with subjects that we know they are passionate about. If it is anger or aggression that is driving their apparent reluctance to engage with the development of mindsets, then trying to understand the reason for this with them may encourage them to come over to our side. And if it is power they are seeking, then we may be able to redirect their energy by giving them a leading role in part of the development strategy.

In order to find out what the main need is that they are trying to fulfil, we can use the skills of coaching (see Chapter 5). This doesn't mean that we are taking a soft approach – in fact, it is the hard thing to do – but at least whatever we decide to do will be from a more informed point of view. One of the true wonders of coaching is that we sometimes find out things about other people that completely shifts our view of them. The important thing is to start with an open mind.

Praise and the words we use

Have you ever said something and regretted it almost immediately? Most of us have and we know from this the immense importance that words can have. On reflection we may have chosen to rephrase what we said. And yet in the classroom we might sometimes say things and use language that we've used on numerous occasions without necessarily thinking too much about it. It may only be when we say something that we immediately sense is wrong that we reflect on it. However, the words we use are part of the drip feed of messages that the pupils receive on a daily basis. And the disturbing thing is, we now know that even things that are said with the express intention of having a positive effect on students can have unforeseen negative consequences. An example of this is our use of praise. Research is now showing us that some forms of praise not only do not support the development of the child or enhance their learning, but can in fact be detrimental to their progress.[3] To illustrate how words used to praise can sometimes backfire on us, let us consider the following situation, the like of which many families will have experienced.

Case study

John and Susan are the parents of three children who have all been through university. Elizabeth is the oldest and she has finished her university studies and now lives in France. William, the middle child, has also finished his degree and is now taking a master's course. Fiona, the youngest of the three, is in her last year at university and is taking various exams that all count towards her final degree grade. Fiona often compares herself with her brother and says things like, 'William's so much more intelligent than me. He didn't have to work hard for his degree and ended up with a first. I will be lucky to get a 2.2.' As caring parents John and Susan clearly want to lift Fiona's self-esteem. The question is, how can this be done?

....

3   See, for example, C. S. Dweck, Caution – praise can be dangerous, *American Educator*, 21(1) (1999), 4–9; and J. Hattie and H. Timperley, The power of feedback, *Review of Educational Research*, 77(1) (2007), 81–112.

Well, an opportunity presents itself when Fiona rings home to tell her parents that she has just received the mark for an exam she took recently and she got the equivalent of 2.1, a grade she's happy with. If you were Fiona's mum or dad what might you say to her? Let's consider two possibilities:

1. You say to her that you're proud of her and this exam result shows clearly how intelligent she really is. In fact, it demonstrates that she is just as intelligent as William.

2. You congratulate her on the effort she must have put in to achieving the result she has got, and you say that the strategies she has used have clearly paid off.

The first option might be tempting. On the face of it, it may seem more personal and caring than the second statement. However, there are real potential problems (unintended consequences) that this could create in the long term.

The next part of the story is that a few weeks later Fiona rings her parents again to say that she's got the result of another exam. This time she's very upset, and tells her mum and dad that she did badly in the exam and only got the equivalent of a third. If her mum and dad had told her previously that they were proud of her for getting such a good grade, how very intelligent she obviously was and it showed that she was just as intelligent as William, what can they say now? How can they help to keep her self-esteem intact? Well, maybe they could comfort her with saying something like, 'It doesn't matter, love – these exams are not so important.' But Fiona will have taken on board what her parents previously said to her, and she may interpret from what they say this time (even if very little is actually said) that her parents are no longer proud of her and no longer think she's intelligent. Even more, for Fiona herself the exams are important and she believes that her mum and dad think they are too, so the fact that her parents now imply that the exams aren't really so important doesn't seem to her to be sincere.

However, if we look at the second statement, it is the effort, techniques and strategies that have been commented on, so when her parents' views of the lower exam grade are given to Fiona it can be the techniques and strategies that are focused on once again. They may now say something like, 'You know you studied very well for the previous exam, Fiona. Can you think of anything you might have done differently in your study programme for this exam?' Now, of course, Fiona might not be in the mood to discuss this at present, but at least it is the studying and effort that is being emphasised in terms of what brings about success.

Our everyday language in schools can at times indicate confusion in our own minds. Many schools talk about ability grouping (whatever this may mean), attainment levels and achievement in the same breath. Highlighting the way in which three things may be conflated is not just about making a semantic point. Much of our language in schools rises up from our subconscious. It is conventional ways of thinking and categorising pupils that will dictate what we do and say, unless we work deliberately to clean up our language.

Let us look a little more at the specific use of praise. For very genuine and well-intentioned reasons there has been a movement in schools to provide as much praise as possible to students. A few years ago it became a mantra for teachers to provide as many positive comments as possible to compensate for any negative statement they needed to utter. Many teachers, with great integrity and good intentions, interpreted this as being given carte blanche to almost blindly give general praise to students. And the more the better. Well, this was certainly an improvement on a culture of criticism and blame that may have existed in some schools, but it carries with it a health warning, as we shall see.

In order to consider the impact that different kinds of praise can have on student learning, we can look at a piece of research carried out by Carol Dweck with hundreds of students.[4] I will split this up into different stages of the procedure.

Stage 1. The students were all given a set of fairly easy problems that they mostly tackled very well.

Stage 2. Afterwards, some students were praised and told that they had done well, and that this clearly showed how smart they were. Others were praised for the effort they had clearly put in to achieving good results. The first group were effectively praised for their special gifts, talent and innate intelligence. The second group were praised for the effort they had put in to arriving at a point where they were successful at solving problems.

---

4   Dweck, *Mindset*, p. 71.

Stage 3. All the students were now given a set of more difficult problems which they were told they could learn a great deal from. Those who had been praised for their ability were reluctant to take on the new task. They were disinclined to attempt something that they might not be able to do because they thought this might reveal that they were not so smart after all. However, the majority (90%) of those students who had been praised for their effort wanted to try the new and challenging task.

Stage 4. All of the students were then given some new problems to do which they all found to be very difficult, and in fact they did not do very well in solving these. Those students who had previously been praised about their ability now thought that they weren't as clever as they had previously thought. There seemed to be a simple equation in their minds:

Success = being intelligent

So it naturally followed that:

Failure = not being intelligent

This is not too hard for us to understand from their point of view and the feedback they had so far been given. On the other hand, the students who had previously been praised for their effort simply felt that they needed to apply more effort to have greater success with the harder problems. They didn't associate their failure with a lack of intelligence. The equation in their minds was quite different:

Success = the result of effort

And it followed that:

Failure = the result of lack of effort

How easy it appears to be for a few words to have such far reaching consequences. The wrong sort of praise can be damaging in terms of how the students approach future work, whereas the right sort of praise can lead to greater persistence in the face of obstacles.

Stage 5. The students were then asked about the level of fun they got from carrying out the different sets of problems. All of the students said they enjoyed the first set of problems. They all did well with these, so to stick with the equation theme for a little longer, you might think that this showed that:

Success = enjoyment

And it follows that:

Failure = lack of enjoyment

This seems logical but it is not strictly true for all the students. When the more difficult problems were attempted, which none of the students did well with, the ability praised students didn't find these fun any more. On the other hand, the effort praised students said they still liked the work and some even said that they found the harder problems to be more fun than the easier ones. Can you believe this? Wouldn't we all like this to be the case with the students that we teach? Remember that at the outset there was no difference between the two sets of students, but a simple variation in the feedback words they were given had altered their view of themselves and the work they were doing.

Stage 6. The most important finding of all was what happened to their future performance. Dweck found that when the students were given another set of questions, similar in standard to the first easier set, the performance of those who had received the ability praise now plummeted. However, the performance of those students who had received the effort praise continued to get better and better. They were using what they had learned from the very hard questions to sharpen their skills and accelerate through the easier problems.

Stage 7. Another somewhat disturbing feature of the study involved the fact that the ability praised students were inclined to lie about their level of success with the problems. They did this on reports that they were told were intended to support other students in tackling the problems. On the report was a small space for them to enter their own marks. Dweck found that 40% of the ability praised students lied about their marks, giving themselves higher scores than they had in fact achieved. Initially praising the children about their ability had turned a number of them into liars!

We can conclude that the dangers in telling students they are smart include:

● They are disinclined to take on challenges that they think they might not be able to do.

● They think they are not clever if they fail.

- They don't find work to be fun if they can't do it.

- They act dumb. They do less well in future work which is similar to other work they have previously done.

- They tend to lie about their ability.

Instead, what we ought to emphasise to students is that they need to work hard, use deliberate practice, work their way through obstacles and employ better strategies.

Dweck found from several experiments with hundreds of children that 'Praising children's intelligence harms their motivation and it harms their performance.'[5] A major challenge for educators in trying not to give praise for an innate quality such as intelligence is that students like receiving it and, if we are honest, we get a pleasure from giving it as well. However, the result is that the student gets a temporary boost, in an analogous way to taking a sugary sweet, but the effect quickly wears off and has a reverse impact once they hit problems.

Should we also refrain from praising students for their success? The answer is emphatically no. Praise can have a positive impact as long as it is not intelligence or talent that we are referring to; rather we should refer to the work and effort that students have put in. So, praise for a growth oriented approach can be given with confidence. Some examples are:

> It's great that you put so much effort into the revision for this test. You deserve the success you have had. Not only that, but this approach will really enable you to grow your knowledge all the time.

> The brilliant thing about all of us is that we have our own ways of doing things. You are now finding the ways of learning that work for you.

> Your ideas in the history essay you wrote showed me how much you had thought about it.

> I hope you feel as good about the effort you have put in to get to this level.

> Your level of concentration on the experiment today was good to see and produced some very impressive results.

----

5   Quoted in M. Syed, The words that could unlock your child, BBC News (19 April 2011). Available at: http://www.bbc.co.uk/news/magazine-13128701.

> You chose a hard subject to write about here. The great thing about this is that it will stretch you and help you to learn so much.

For students who work hard but don't get great results, Dweck suggests that it is important to still give them messages that help them to focus on the positives and what they might try next time. For example:

> You know, it's not the things that you found easy earlier on this year that will help your brain to grow and help you to learn. This may be harder work for you right now, but it will start to make sense when you really work at it.
>
> Okay, let's have a look together at what you might try that could help with this.
>
> Sometimes being able to focus on the things that we don't at first understand helps us to think of what we might do to overcome a challenge. Why don't we see if we can find out what these things are and then try ways of tackling each of them one at a time?

Let's now take an example of a student, let's call her Amanda, who has not done well in a school maths test. As her teacher, what message might we relay back to her? (I have adapted the following to fit into a school context from an example given by Dweck of feedback given by a parent to a child.[6]) The options are:

1. Tell Amanda that she deserved to do well.

2. Tell Amanda that the test was hard and didn't allow her to show her ability.

3. Tell Amanda that maths is not such an important thing in the big scheme of things.

4. Tell Amanda that she has real ability in maths and will do well next time.

5. Tell Amanda that the results she got are a fair reflection of her present position in maths.

As teachers, we may feel at times that we need to preserve the self-esteem of students by protecting them from failure. We may even feel pressure from society as a whole, and possibly even the school leadership, to do this. Dweck says that although this will help the student to overcome disappointment in the short term,

....

6   Dweck, *Mindset*, p. 180.

it can have negative longer term consequences.[7] We can consider each option in turn and the potential consequences from a mindset point of view.

1. There is no indication here for the student of how to improve. Can we be sure that she deserved to do well? This message might seem very insincere to Amanda.

2. Amanda might get the message that success in exams is about the luck of the draw, and that she would have succeeded with an easier test but is not up to tackling hard tests. She may start to blame external factors for any lack of success in her life.

3. Surely, we don't want to make Amanda feel that maths is not important to her.

4. How do we know that she will do well? It will depend on a number of things, not least of all her approach to working to improve. It implies that ability will get you there. Will Amanda interpret ability as an innate talent? If she does then she may wonder why she should work hard to improve for next time.

5. This may seem harsh but it gives a clear message. You would, of course, want to add more to it and maybe use slightly different words, but the message is the same: we now know your current situation. You would then go on to talk to Amanda about the steps she might now take to move from this current situation towards reaching her goal – perhaps something like this:

   > Amanda, I can imagine that you are feeling disappointed and perhaps upset. This is natural. No one succeeds at everything in the way that they would like at the first attempt. It depends now on how well you wish to do next time and whether you are prepared to do the work necessary to improve in the maths that this kind of test is looking at. You have the potential within you to constantly improve if you are prepared to work at it.

The message to Amanda is now clear. It is that hard work will bring success, and it is not about some intrinsic weakness in her. If she is happy to stay at the standard she is at then that is her decision, but if she wants to improve she knows what she

---

7   Dweck, *Mindset*, p. 181.

has to do. You might talk to her initially about how she can learn from this experience and then go on to explore with her the possibilities that will lead to greater success. The message here is that simply withholding the truth from students does not support their long-term growth. Protecting children from reality harms them and does not help them to learn. Students need honest and constructive feedback.

Another interesting situation to consider is what to say when students complete work quickly and with apparent ease. The question here is, should we praise them with comments like, 'That is impressive – you did that in no time and without any mistakes'? Dweck strongly suggests that we should not do this because it gives students the message that we are placing an emphasis on both speed and perfection.[8] This will lead them to think that they shouldn't try anything that is a challenge for them, that might take time and that they might not do perfectly, because this would send a signal that they are no longer smart. So what do we say? Well, Dweck suggests comments like, 'I'm sorry, that was too easy for you. I apologise for wasting your time. Let's do something that you can really learn from.'

Here are some more messages that you may wish to consider, adapt and then practise before using with your students:

- You know, sometimes work can seem tedious but we can use this as an opportunity to find new ways to concentrate. Let's see how well you can concentrate on this …

- This may seem like a boring piece of work to do, so we need to think of ways to make it more interesting. How can you make this more fun to do and still produce great results?

- Let's look together at what you might not understand at the moment so that you can then decide on your next step which will help you to make good progress.

- You may be finding this hard at the moment but this is the very time when you will learn most. Easy stuff teaches us little or nothing.

....

8   Dweck, *Mindset*, p. 179.

- The challenge in learning is that it can be unpleasant at times. Just like in sport, we only improve by stretching ourselves and this can feel uncomfortable while we are doing it.

We need to help students to understand their present situation and then support them in finding the tools to close the gap between this and their goal. We should never judge them but be consistent in the messages that we give about the learning process. The aim is to foster an interest in learning in the students that supports their continual growth. As teachers we are in a very privileged position – and, yes, a very challenging position at the same time. Teaching gives us the opportunity to learn about other people, life and ourselves. By resisting the temptation to comment on the intelligence or talent of students, we are able to focus our energy on the process of learning, which includes the strategies used, the effort employed and the choices made by the students.

Developing a growth mindset in students allows us to support them to fulfil their potential. We need to keep expectations and standards high while at the same time providing them with the kinds of strategies, techniques and methods which will allow them to constantly improve. Changing mindsets can take time and effort. Sometimes it is not a case of simply replacing one mindset with another but rather the two living side by side, and then, with practice, the growth mindset beginning to become the dominant way of thinking, feeling and behaving. As this happens their internal dialogue will become less judgemental and more focused on using the information they receive to help them move forward. They will gradually stop saying to themselves things like, 'I'm hopeless at this' or 'This shows how brilliant I am', and move to a more constructive appraisal of their present situation, their goals and the steps they need to take to achieve these goals.

It is never their intention to do so, but schools can sometimes make students feel as if the fixed mindset view of life rules and is dominant. In other words, students can begin to develop a fixed mindset about their ability to achieve. For all students this can lead to a self-fulfilling prophecy. The students who consider themselves to be a failure may ask themselves, 'Why should I try when I know I'm no good?' The student who believes they are average will also tend to self-regulate at the level at which they think they operate – not trying too hard but just enough to keep themselves in the middle. Even the students who think they are clever can suffer from this fixed mindset mentality: when things are going well they are reassured that their view of themselves is correct – they are clever and their results show this. But when obstacles are met they begin to doubt themselves. They may say, 'Perhaps I'm not as clever as I thought I was', and begin to act accordingly.

Three versions of a fixed mindset

Some people may say that it is part of life that some of us succeed while others fail, and that students need to know where they stand because this is the real world. It is true to say that we need to give feedback to students that reflects the reality of their current learning at any given time. But it should also be made clear to them that this is simply a snapshot of their present performance and does not in itself predict or secure future results. Then we can move them into a growth mindset where it is effort that secures success and not some predetermined talent (or lack of it). Thomas Edison is reported to have said, 'Genius is one per cent inspiration and ninety-nine per cent perspiration.' This is something that we must promote with the students we teach.

You may even hear teachers, perhaps in the staffroom, unintentionally promoting the notion of fixed mindsets by saying things like, 'John is really clever' or 'I don't think Peter will ever achieve very much in my subject.' This is not just lazy language but it is also very dangerous language. If these beliefs are held by teachers then they will ooze out of them in their interactions with the students. They may claim that they would never say these things directly to the students (and this may be true) but their beliefs will nevertheless impact on their behaviour towards students, even if this is at a subconscious level.

To be as successful as possible in promoting a growth mindset in students, educators must reflect on their own mindsets, as I have made clear on a number of occasions in this book. The point is that if we don't have a growth mindset and believe in an individual's ability to constantly grow, then we are unlikely to be able to foster this in the students we teach. You might wish to use the following affirmation that will support your development of a growth mindset:

> I believe that we all have the capacity to develop our personal intelligence. It is fundamentally effort rather than innate giftedness that determines the success of people in life.

A word of warning about 'you are's

In general 'you are's are very dangerous, whether we are describing something negative or positive about a student. The reason for this is that we are identifying something about them that gives the impression to them that this is fixed. However, there are a few 'you are's that we can use that can work well. These include:

> You are a multi-dimensional, complex person who can develop in ways that neither I, you nor anyone else can fully appreciate at the moment.

> You are a person with a potential that is both unknown and unknowable.

> You are a person who has more potential connections in your brain, which collectively represent your learning, than has ever been utilised by anyone in the history of humankind.

> You are a person with the richest resource that you will ever find lying right inside you, waiting to be cared for, nurtured, grown, matured and fully utilised. This resource is your brain.

Now, you may wish to alter the wording of these to suit your particular student audience, but the principles in these statements should remain the same. The fact is that they all apply to each and every individual you teach. All adults in the school should try to adopt these beliefs, possibly through affirmations, so they become a natural way for them to think.

Motivation rules OK

We are all aware that motivation is essential to the success of all that we do and it is a key part of our EI. If students are not motivated, they will never achieve all they are capable of. Motivation from the outside of the person (extrinsic motivation) can be important in getting them to kick start an activity. It can maintain a level of commitment to something as long as the motivational force remains. Rewards can act as (extrinsic) motivators but they can also backfire; there can be a hidden cost (unexpected consequence) of a reward, as we will now explore.

The 'overjustification effect' describes how adding an extrinsic motivator, like a prize, to something that a person already feels intrinsically motivated to do can result in the intrinsic motivation being diminished. An example of this effect was found in an experiment carried out by Mark Lepper, David Greene and Richard Nisbett in 1973.[9] They went to a nursery where they found, unsurprisingly, many children happily involved and interested in various activities during a fun-time session, and some of them were clearly very much enjoying doing drawing and colouring activities. For the purposes of the experiment they divided these budding artists into three groups: the expected award group, the unexpected award group and the no award group.

<table>
<tr><td>A</td><td>B</td><td>C</td></tr>
<tr><td>Expected award</td><td>Unexpected award</td><td>No award</td></tr>
</table>

....

9 M. P. Lepper, D. Greene and R. E. Nisbett, Undermining children's intrinsic interest with extrinsic reward: a test of the 'overjustification' hypothesis, *Journal of Personality and Social Psychology*, 28(1) (1973), 129–137.

Children in the expected award group were told that if they continued with their drawing and colouring in the next fun-time session they would be given a certificate with a beautiful ribbon around it. Children in the unexpected award group were offered nothing, but if they continued to draw and colour they were given a certificate identical to the children in the expected award group. The children in the no award group were also offered nothing, and even if they continued to draw and colour they still did not receive an award. The researchers then returned two weeks later to observe the children as they were given the same choice of activities as they had been given before the experiment took place. What do you imagine they found in the way that the three groups of children now performed?

The researchers found that children in the unexpected award group and the no award group continued to enjoy the art activities. However, the expected award group did not. It was almost as if they were different people now. They spent significantly less time carrying out the art activities than the children in the other two groups. The researchers concluded that the expected reward diminished the intrinsic motivation of the children. It appears that the children in the expected award group concluded that the reward was there because the task must be something that was not necessarily desirable to do. Therefore, when the reward was removed they stopped doing the task.

As we start to work with pupils on developing a growth mindset, we are trying at the same time to develop inside them the motivation to want to learn (intrinsic motivation). There are various theories about motivation, but one that seems to make a lot of sense to me is what I refer to as the AMP golden triangle of motivation. For most of us motivation involves three key components: autonomy, mastery and purpose – or AMP. *Autonomy* is about students feeling that they have control over their learning. *Mastery* is about students constantly moving towards greater levels of competency in a given activity. They can achieve this, of course, through deliberate practice. *Purpose* occurs when the students feel that they are involved in learning that has a greater value than just the specific piece of learning itself. We all work best when what we are doing supports something that we believe in.

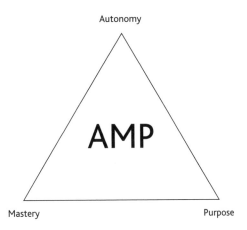

Highly effective educators build a classroom and school environment where these dimensions are part of the normal way things operate. Pupils are given frequent opportunities to take ownership of their learning, scaffold their own learning to ever greater levels of mastery and see that their learning has meaning for them both now and in the future. We know that motivation works best when we want to do something rather than feeling that we have to do something. It may seem self-evident but if we can get pupils to want to learn (intrinsic motivation) rather than having to somehow force them to learn (extrinsic motivation) then we are on to a real winner.

However, we know that with the best will in the world we can provide pupils with a lot of AMP opportunities and their motivation may still not seem to improve. So what do we do then? Well, one of the ways of energising students to learn, and trigger their intrinsic motivation, is by finding out a little more about the true nature of their present motivation in any given learning activity. Once we understand something about their motivation we can begin to support them to fully utilise their motivation to help their learning. The very fact that the students understand that we are interested in what motivates them will in itself be a great motivator.

As we have already seen, intrinsic motivation is an internal process, but it can be significantly influenced by external circumstances. Many of us will have experienced situations where our state has been almost instantly altered by what someone has said to us. This may put us into a positive 'can do' mode of thinking or alternatively make us feel less confident about carrying out a task. We need to be constantly aware of this and create a classroom culture and climate that brings out the very best in learners. The following section describes how we can gather valuable information that we can then share with the students to support their motivation and learning.

The expectancy–value model

If some of your students have a fixed mindset about learning, you can use the following model to work with them to encourage them to understand that they have great capability inside of them. The aim is to shift their level of *expectancy* about whether they are able to achieve a particular goal in a piece of learning. Another factor that could come into play, of course, is the degree to which they *value* any success they may get from the effort they put into the learning. Some students will simply not see the point in learning something, even if they believe that they can do it. Putting these two factors together creates what is sometimes referred to as the expectancy–value model. I have found this simplified form to be useful in schools.

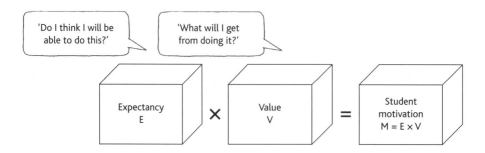

We can use coaching with the pupils to find out from them about their levels of expectancy of success (E) and the value they place on the activity (V). I use a rating scale of 0 to 10 with students to represent their subjective sense of their own E and V as a numerical score. The outcome of E and V gives us a motivational percentage (M). In my experience, the process involved in discussing with the pupils the extent to which they expect to be able to succeed if they put in the effort, and the value they place on succeeding, is far more valuable than the numerical number for their motivation, although you may wish to get values for E, V and M for a whole class before you embark on a specific piece of classroom learning. The great thing about this model is that you can use it right now with your students to help them and you to understand more about their motivation. For young children you may wish to modify the language a little but this can be done very easily.

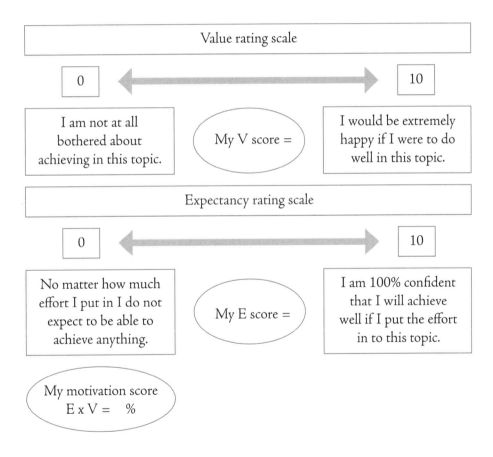

Start off by giving the students a copy of the expectancy and value rating scales above. Remember to emphasise to them that you are doing this with them in partnership. In no way is it a test: your motives are completely honourable and are about supporting their learning in the best way you possibly can. It is also important that you should view the feedback you get in a thoroughly professional way and not feel that it is a reflection on you as a person. However, you must be prepared to act on the information you gather to make the exercise as useful as possible.

Let us look at some potential results you might get. At the beginning of the year you might ask the students in your class to complete a motivation questionnaire concerning their expectancy to do well in your subject (or a subject) and the value they place on doing well. As a rule of thumb, a score of 50% or above is good. The following results are from some of the class members.

Layali gives scores of:

(My E score = 3) X (My V score = 10) = (My M score E x V = 30%)

What action might you take? (Try to answer this and the following examples before looking at the suggestions on the next page.)

Peter gives scores of:

(My E score = 9) X (My V score = 2) = (My M score E x V = 18%)

Anne gives scores of:

(My E score = 9) X (My V score = 9) = (My M score E x V = 81%)

Shireen gives scores of:

$$\left(\text{My E score} = 2\right) \quad \text{x} \quad \left(\text{My V score} = 2\right) \quad = \quad \left(\begin{array}{c}\text{My M score}\\ \text{E x V} = 4\%\end{array}\right)$$

Saad gives scores of:

$$\left(\text{My E score} = 5\right) \quad \text{x} \quad \left(\text{My V score} = 5\right) \quad = \quad \left(\begin{array}{c}\text{My M score}\\ \text{E x V} = 25\%\end{array}\right)$$

Here are some reflections on the findings from the expectancy–value motivation questionnaire results.

Layali E = 3 V = 10 E x V = 30%	Layali's desire to do well is high because she has given a very high value score (V = 10). You therefore do not need to overly convince her of the value of doing well in the subject. However, her expectancy to do well is low (E = 3). You would therefore want to encourage her to develop a belief in her ability. You might ask her coaching questions, as described in this book, that seek out more information about why her expectancy is so low. She may well have developed a fixed mindset which needs to be addressed.
Peter E = 9 V = 2 E x V = 18%	Peter has a strong belief that if he tries he will do well (E = 9) but he places very little importance on doing well (V = 2). Whenever you see a low value score you have to think about how you might 'sell' this topic more effectively to this student. Essentially, if they don't buy into the importance of putting effort into the topic then they will not be fully motivated to learn it either. Again, further coaching questions with the student will definitely improve the chances of finding a way forward in supporting them.
Anne E = 9 V = 9 E x V = 81%	On the face of it everything seems rosy with Anne. Her motivation level is very high both in terms of her level of expectancy that she will do well and the level of importance she feels about the topic. However, your task is to maintain this high level. As with all the students, continuous messages about the importance of having a growth mindset will pay dividends in terms of the student's learning.

Shireen $E = 2$ $V = 2$ $E \times V = 4\%$	If Shireen is giving us figures that truly reflect her beliefs here, then we have significant work to do both in terms of raising her expectancy that she can do well and the value that she places on this. It may well be that one of these beliefs is impacting on the other. Coaching her will reveal more about this, and giving her clear growth mindset messages will also be of great benefit. We know that low levels of confidence are linked with poor motivation. From the coaching you do with her you might discover that this is the case with Shireen. Research shows that if we can develop positive self-regard in our students, greater motivation will follow.
Saad $E = 5$ $V = 5$ $E \times V = 25\%$	Saad would appear to have average levels for both aspects of his motivation but we can see that the combined effect of these gives him a low score of 25%. We can adopt a similar approach as that used with Shireen. From early discussions with Saad we might then begin to understand the actions that we (both Saad and ourselves) might need to take in order to begin to raise his overall level of motivation.

You can use an expectancy–value motivation questionnaire like this at various times of the year to check on how the motivation levels of the students might have changed concerning the subject as a whole. You can also use it in terms of specific topics that you cover. It is important to make it clear to your students that real motivation comes from within, but that you want to help them in any way you can. This process should help you to build up a highly positive relationship with your class where the learning that takes place is part of a constructive partnership between you and the students.

It should also be noted that a number of studies have shown that boys, more so than girls, tend to report higher levels of academic confidence than would be justified objectively.[10] This may therefore elevate the expectancy scores of boys compared to girls. Likewise, when I introduce the expectancy–value model to teachers they sometimes ask whether the rankings provided by the students can be relied on. These are, of course, valid concerns. This process is not scientific, nor is it intended to be. The exercise is very subjective, with numbers attached to it to provide a way of analysing the feedback and to provide a source of discussion with

....

10 See J. Hattie and G. Yates, *Visible Learning and the Science of How We Learn* (Abingdon and New York: Routledge, 2014), p. 215.

the students. The greatest benefit comes from the discussion around the scores they have provided and not the scores themselves.

We all have a responsibility to try to ignite the passion for learning within the students we teach. You, like me, will no doubt recall certain key individuals throughout the course of your own education who had a positive influence on you. They may even have been instrumental in you deciding to become a teacher or classroom support assistant. Consider for a moment whether they motivated you to learn. Well, the truth is that if they ignited something inside of you that triggered a chain reaction that resulted in a great motivation to learn then they may well have acted as a catalyst for your motivation. But long-lasting motivation comes from what lies inside a person. Once again, this is the intrinsic motivation that involves us in wanting to do something. Extrinsic motivation can sometimes cause us to act, but it is often because we have to do it rather than that we want to do it.

Most people enjoy going on holidays, so they are motivated to think about where they will go next. However, many people (I am certainly speaking from personal experience here) will not be highly motivated by the idea of cleaning their kitchen. They will feel that they have to do it for a whole variety of reasons. However, motivation is very much an individual thing. What one person feels intrinsically motivated to do, another person will only do if there are external forces that provide them with extrinsic motivation. And so it is with students. If they want to do something they will be filled with intrinsic motivation to complete the activity. If they don't want to do something then they may still complete the activity if they think that they have no choice. (The classic case is a student saying to a teacher, 'Do I really have to do this?' and the teacher replying, 'Yes, it's on your syllabus.' This response is unlikely to ignite much intrinsic motivation in most students.)

Our success as teachers is largely determined by our ability to stimulate intrinsic motivation in our students. But one danger that we must be aware of is not to label students as either 'motivated' or 'unmotivated'. Labelling is something that is very easy to do and in many ways school systems are set up in such a way that it can be hard not to do this. For example, in the examples above, it would be very easy for a teacher to think that Layali is highly motivated and Peter is demotivated, but it would be wrong to do this and at the same time untrue. The fact is that both Layali and Peter are motivated to do various things. At the moment Layali is displaying the motivation to learn at school whereas Peter is not. However, Peter, like Layali, will have great motivation in a whole range of things: he may be learning many things outside of school and some of them may be quite inspirational. Of course, some of them might not be wholly beneficial to his development and long-term well-being, but this could be equally as true of Layali. The point is that we are all motivated in different ways.

Our job is to try to find out how we can ignite the students to want to learn both in school and for the rest of their lives. But how can we tap into their intrinsic motivation? Well, one of the critical things that students need to feel is that a teacher believes in them. This includes a belief that the student can succeed, has great potential and has certain qualities that are very worthy. A great video about a teacher's beliefs was made by the Ministry of Education in Singapore.[11] It is based on a true story and features two people, Mrs Chong (the teacher) and Edwin (the student). I will leave it for you to watch but the key message is about the belief that Mrs Chong continues to have in Edwin, even when his life takes a bad turn. It finishes with the messages: 'You never forget a good teacher' and 'TEACH. You'll be amazed at the difference you can make.' I have shown this to teachers in a number of countries during training sessions and in many cases it has reduced them to tears. So be warned!

If you ask students they will tell you what makes a good teacher and a lot of this will be about how the teacher has motivated and inspired them. In 2000, the Hay McBer group produced a report for the then Department for Education and Employment called *Research into Teacher Effectiveness*,[12] which is well worth reading. Hay McBer asked students what they thought made a good teacher. This was what some Year 8 students said:

A good teacher ...

is kind

is generous

---

11 See https://www.youtube.com/watch?v=sPROyH3iw90.

12 Hay McBer, *Research into Teacher Effectiveness: A Model of Teacher Effectiveness*. Research report no. 216 (Norwich: DfEE/HMSO, 2000). Available at: http://webarchive.nationalarchives.gov.uk/20130401151715/http://www.education.gov.uk/publications/eorderingdownload/rr216.pdf.

listens to you

encourages you

has faith in you

keeps confidences

likes teaching children

likes teaching their subject

takes time to explain things

helps you when you're stuck

tells you how you are doing

allows you to have your say

doesn't give up on you

cares for your opinion

makes you feel clever

treats people equally

stands up for you

makes allowances

tells the truth

is forgiving.[13]

These are definitely qualities found in exceptional teachers and classroom support assistants. And all of these qualities are used by great educators to develop intrinsic motivation in students.

Another useful model to help us understand student motivation is Abraham Maslow's hierarchy of needs. This was proposed by Maslow in his 1943 paper 'A theory of human motivation',[14] and it has stood the test of time. Maslow believed that human motivation is based on people seeking fulfilment and change for personal growth. The levels are as follows:

13 Hay McBer, *Research into Teacher Effectiveness*, p. 3.

14 A. Maslow, A theory of human motivation, *Psychological Review*, 50(4) (1943), 370–396.

How to change the mindsets of a school community

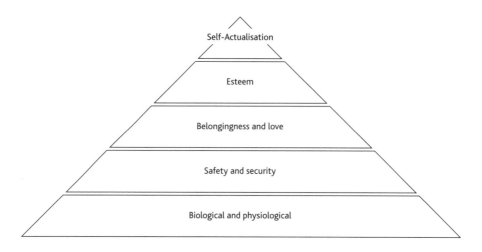

- Level 1: Biological and physiological needs. This is our most basic level. We are motivated to want things such as air, food, drink, shelter, warmth, sex and sleep.

- Level 2: Safety and security needs. We desire to have protection from the elements. In addition, we seek things such as security, a sense of order, protection through the law, understandable limits and relative stability.

- Level 3: Belongingness and love needs. Many of us are able to satisfy this need through our family, friends, work colleagues and other relationships.

- Level 4: Esteem needs. Now we move into the level where we seek self-esteem through things such as achievement at work, mastery of a skill, achieving some independence, status from our work and the feeling that we are making a difference that matters.

- Level 5: Self-actualisation needs. This is the highest level and it is where we achieve a true sense of fulfilment. It is where we are exercising high levels of our personal potential, our dreams are being realised, we experience personal growth, we have a sense of authentic self-mastery, we are able to exercise our creativity and we may feel a sense of connecting with something bigger than ourselves and the activity itself.

In our lives we might oscillate up and down the hierarchy. For example, if we lose our job then we might be thrown into a state where fulfilling the lower two levels occupies our time at the expense of the upper three levels. It is also important to be aware that self-actualisation is an ongoing process. It is not a perfect state to be reached of a 'happy ever after'.

Great schools and great teachers provide elements for students at all five of these levels. A key idea behind the hierarchy is that a lower level need must be satisfied before progressing on to the next higher level. However, Maslow accepted that the order in which these needs are fulfilled does not always follow a rigid progression. For some people, the need for self-esteem is more important than the need for love. For others, the need for creative fulfilment at the self-actualisation level may be pursued at the expense of some of the more basic needs. But if for a moment we accept the normal progression process up the hierarchy, along with the possibility that a lot of deep learning is operating at the highest self-actualisation level, then we can reflect on and understand why some students may not be engaged with learning in our classes in the way that we would like them to be. This model reminds us that the physical, emotional, social and intellectual dimensions of an individual will all impact on their learning.

In a study conducted by Dr Benjamin Bloom of the University of Chicago, he asked 21 internationally accomplished pianists to describe their very first piano teachers.[15] The following are some of the comments he received:

> She was very kindly, very nice.
>
> He was enormously patient and not very pushy.
>
> It was an event for me to go to my lessons.

These teachers were igniting passion and motivation. Bloom said: 'The effect of this first phase of learning seemed to be to get the learner involved, captivated, hooked, and to get the learner to need and want more information and expertise.'[16] Motivation is an essential element for a school moving towards a mindset for success.

....

15 Quoted in Coyle, *The Talent Code*, pp. 172 and 175.

16 Quoted in D. Brooks, *The Social Animal: The Hidden Sources of Love, Character, and Achievement* (London: Short Books, 2012), p. 102.

In this chapter, we have looked at some of the important models we can use to help us understand the motivation of our students. We can use these to gain an appreciation of what motivates individual students, and as a result to adopt strategies that can support them in developing higher levels of intrinsic motivation.

Some key action points on motivation

1. Completing the expectancy–value motivation questionnaire takes very little time. However, you will need to prepare the students for this by introducing them to the importance of motivation in all that we do in life and the purpose of them completing the questionnaire. You can tell the students that their answers will not be shared with anyone else in the class, unless you feel that there is some benefit in opening up a discussion about motivation. The real benefit, as mentioned above, will come from the dialogue that this will open up for you with them. Students value the interaction and feedback received from teachers they respect.

2. You can provide opportunities for students to develop their motivation and self-esteem in a variety of ways. These include:

   - Enabling the students to work independently.

   - Highlighting when the students are showing how they are advancing their learning.

   - Providing challenging but attainable tasks in which the students are proud to achieve success.

3. There are a number of ways that you can provide a sense of self-actualisation for the students. As a starting point you might think about these:

   - Making great use of their present abilities. A teacher who gets to know their students will become aware of these abilities and assist them to use these fully.

   - Enabling them to feel a sense of identity.

- Giving opportunities for them to carry out creative tasks. Some students will believe that they are not creative, but with a growth mindset view a teacher can encourage creativity in all of their students.

- Providing opportunities to have fun through exploration. Encourage students to try to fail at times. Failure provides learning experiences and, ultimately, great fulfilment.

- Providing opportunities for them to achieve in things that they really value. As you carry out coaching work on the expectancy–value motivation questionnaire, the students will give you feedback on what they value.

The challenge of sustainability

In general, are you an initiator of ideas or someone who likes to take something through to fruition? Do you like chairing meetings, providing detailed knowledge and monitoring the progress of a new initiative, or do you like spending time with individuals in a team so that they work closely together? These are very different roles, and it is important in a school for there to be a clear understanding of the responsibilities people have for ensuring that the mindset for success initiative has sustainability. You may be the one who initiates the programme, but are you the best person to ensure it is kept high on the agenda, monitored for its effectiveness and carried forward to its final stage?

I know from the schools that I work with that there have been concerns about how to maintain the level of success that has been experienced in the first year. Considerations may include: what will happen if the head teacher moves on to another school or retires? What will happen if the key person responsible for mindsets in the school leaves? What about the impact that comes from having a turnover of staff? How do we deal with new children and their parents coming into the school who may not know anything about the ideas behind mindsets? All of these factors should ideally be part of a development plan for mindsets.

The reality is that not everything in the initial plan may come to fruition because of time issues, among many other things. But being proactive at the outset will save a lot of time and increase the probability of success and sustainability in the long term. The evidence tells us that the head teacher in any school has an enormous impact on the organisational culture. It is impossible to be certain that a mindsets culture in a school will survive the arrival of a new head teacher who understandably comes along with new thoughts and priorities. However, there will be a greater likelihood of this if the school has achieved a tipping point where the tide of influence has moved towards a culture of growth mindsets. This is one of the obvious reasons why all members of the school community should be involved in the training. Of course, a measure of great leadership is the level at which the success in the school is maintained once the leader leaves, and this is highly dependent on the capacity building that supports sustainability.

A plan that works

From my experience, a number of essential elements are required to embed a mindset for success in a school.

Once I have had initial discussions with the head teacher and other key members of the school to establish a commitment from them, the first step is for the school to complete what I call a school focus and goal setting plan (see Appendix A). This enables the school to be absolutely clear about the desired outcome of the mindset for success programme. I ask the school to decide on the major goal and a series of sub-goals, all of which should satisfy the SMARTER conditions. (As a reminder, SMARTER stands for specific, measurable, achievable, realistic, time bound, energising and rewarding – see Chapter 5.) In addition, I ask the school to consider the key benefits that they will get from a successful outcome, the barriers that may present themselves and how they think they can overcome these barriers. The RAS of each individual in the school should be alerted to ways of achieving the goals so that there is a collective focus and alignment on what the school is intending to achieve.

The next stage is for a mindset for success programme to be established with the content and dates agreed upon. The programme should include training for each group within the school – teachers, support staff, pupils, parents and governors. It is important that the package should be bespoke to the requirements of the school (an example plan can be found in Appendix B). For instance, I have found that some schools want to incorporate coaching training within the mindset for success programme, while other schools choose to focus on the key findings of visible learning and link these with the key elements of mindsets. In other cases where, for example, maths is proving to be a subject that the students are struggling with, this can be focused on throughout the training. Another important part of the plan for many schools is for action research to be carried out by a number of staff. The action research should be something that the individual or group of staff have a real interest in. (We will return to the topic of action research in Chapter 9.)

The plan gives structure to the training that will take place, but it is also important that there is flexibility so any particular priorities that become apparent throughout the training can be woven into the programme. I normally recommend that the mindset for success programme should be continued over a period of 12 months so that staff and parents have the chance to absorb the ideas and make adjustments, first of all in their own minds and then in their actions. This is essential if it is to feed through to the pupils with consistency and clarity. Culture change does not happen overnight and the drip feed that brings about the changes that are desired must be repeated and reinforced over a period of time.

Although I have been an external trainer for different schools, working with them to develop a growth mindset culture, it is perfectly possible for a member of staff in the school to take on this role as long as they have reached a high level of knowledge concerning mindsets and have the necessary credibility in the eyes of all members of the school to successfully carry out the training. If this is the case then a plan like the one I have described here could be used by the member of staff. What works less well is one or two twilight training sessions, or even a full training day, spent on mindsets, unless there is significant ongoing input for all members of the school to reinforce the messages delivered during the training. The reason for this is that changing people's habits, attitudes and beliefs takes time. Adults in the school will need time for reflection and to try out ideas – sometimes unsuccessfully but always with learning – before true change takes place. I sometimes refer to KASH to explain that for mindset change to take place it requires at least four elements: *knowledge, attitude, skills* and *habits*. We can provide information about mindsets through training which allows people to acquire knowledge, but they then have to implement this through deliberate practice which develops their skills. However, for real success people need to have the time to reflect on their own attitudes and habits, which may need to be modified in order for them to embrace a new approach to learning. This applies equally to the adults in the school as well as to the parents and children.

In the next chapter we will look at why action research on mindsets can be very powerful, what action research is all about, how to carry out action research and some of the possibilities you may look at for action research in your school.

Chapter 9
The benefits of action research

Why action research?

Some of the schools I have worked with have decided to incorporate action research on mindsets into their action development plan. This can range from one teacher to a whole team of people who are working on different areas of mindsets in the school. There are distinct advantages to adopting an action research approach. These are:

- **Reflective practitioners.** It helps us all to become ever more equipped as reflective practitioners. No teacher has ever reached the pinnacle of what it is possible for them to do in the classroom; if anybody has ever thought they have then they would be adopting a fixed mindset approach. Outstanding teachers are always looking to improve what they do presently, otherwise complacency can set in and the danger of declining effectiveness can result. Being a reflective practitioner is about reaching the level of reflective competence mentioned in Chapter 3. It is about being a leader and attempting to become ever more effective at what we do, rather than adopting a more management-based approach where we might be carrying out things very efficiently, and which once worked for us, but we are no longer producing the same. In terms of mindsets, action research enables us to be reflective practitioners about some of the things that are going to make the biggest difference to the learning and the lives of the students we teach.

- **Whole-school priorities.** If developing mindsets in the school has been determined to be something of great importance, then action research will enable a focused effort to be placed on certain critical aspects which the school has identified.

- **Building professional cultures.** We have already considered how important it is to create a culture where growth mindsets are part of the accepted norm. Action research can help to support the development of a culture which believes in the enormous potential that lies within each individual, where endeavour is emphasised and encouraged, and where grit and resilience are constantly nurtured. It also helps the school to develop as a learning community within which there are small and large communities of adult learners.

What is action research?

Effective educators, teachers and support staff are constantly reflecting on the things they do, whether what they are doing are the right things and how they might do things even better in the future. Action research is a way of making this process more structured. So, in a disciplined way, a teacher, classroom support assistant or other member of staff in the school may decide to carry out an enquiry into a particular aspect of school life with the aim that whatever is found out will benefit them, potentially other people in the school and maybe other people in other schools as well. The main focus has to be on improving practice, so the action research should be relevant to the individual(s) carrying out the research. Relevance should always be key because the particular piece of research is decided upon by the researcher themselves, and they will be the principal beneficiary of the findings. The main aim of the research should be that the researcher finds out how to become ever more effective in terms of their teaching, the students' learning and the broad development of the students.

Action research also supports the professionalisation of teaching, as well as acting as a motivator for many staff as they search for new ways of meeting the learning needs of a wide spectrum of students. Society is not homogeneous and no student body is homogeneous either. Therefore, the great challenge we have as educators is to provide for many different needs within each child's unique universe. This could be thought of as an insurmountable barrier (the LOC is outside us) or we can treat it as a wonderful and exciting challenge (by keeping the LOC firmly inside us). Action researchers can be like detectives in their own classrooms, constantly striving to find the answer to continually changing and challenging puzzles. Within the structure of what we are asked to teach, there is no way that teachers can be successful if we act like robots implementing a curriculum through an outdated approach to classroom practice. And, indeed, none of us would get any satisfaction from adopting this kind of methodology. Action research allows us to take back control and endeavour to find those wonderful and sometimes elusive practices that make such a difference to the learning and lives of the students.

Most teachers enter the profession because they want to make a difference. As time goes by the pressures faced by teachers as a result of a multitude of competing demands may wear down even the most committed. The demands of the classroom have always been there, but changes in society, increasing demands from parents, financial cutbacks and centralised insistence on a target driven emphasis in schools can all create a sense of overload. One of the things I say to the teachers I work with is that a focus on mindsets can bring us back to the core ideology we have about education. Action research enables teachers to investigate those things that really do make a difference to the students, and therefore reinvigorate them with a genuine sense of self-efficacy and the desire to take back the LOC which they might have allowed to slip away from them. The knowledge that the hard work we put in as teachers is paying real dividends can be a very significant energising force for all of us.

How do I carry out action research?

When educators carry out action research the process of them reflecting on their current practice and how this can be improved is often as beneficial as the findings themselves. A model that I have created and that seems to help people structure their research is called the GROWN model. This is very much a solution focused approach to action research.

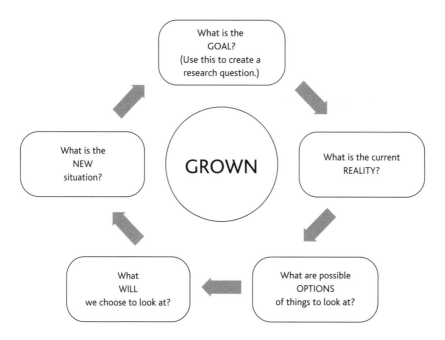

I created the GROWN model because it seems sensible to align action research with another model that is used in coaching called the GROW model (see Chapter 5). GROWN stands for *goal*, *reality*, *options*, *will* and *new*, and it works as follows.

Goal

The question to be asked here is, 'What is the goal?' This enables a focus for the research to be identified. Within this stage it is also important to determine the precise wording of the research question.

Reality

The question to be asked here is, 'What is the current reality?' In other words, what is the thing, that we wish to investigate, like at the moment? In many cases with action research, we may be trying something new and looking for the impact that this has on learning. However, it is impossible to know with certainty what the full impact of any intervention has been without having a level of clarity about the situation before we implement any action. Therefore, the reality stage involves collecting and analysing current data. It may be either quantitative (objective and often involving numbers) or qualitative (subjective and often involving gathering people's views and thoughts) or a mixture of both. The information and knowledge gained from the reality stage can be used to modify, if necessary, the research question set out in the goal stage.

Options

The question to be asked here is, 'What are possible options of things to look at?' or 'What potential things might I do to change the current reality and move towards my goal?' At this stage it is not about deciding on the specific actions to be taken, but rather thinking through a variety of possibilities. Once again, reflection on the options stage may well result in a modification of the research question set out in the goal stage.

Will

The question to be asked here is, 'What will we choose to look at?' or 'Which of the potential options I have looked at do I want to focus on?' This then determines precisely what the researcher will take action on.

New

The question to be asked here is, 'What is the new situation?' or 'What is the new reality?' In other words, what is the situation like now? How has the thing that we are looking at changed? This will involve collecting and analysing the data so that we can then compare this with the original reality. An analysis of the difference between the new and current reality stages enables us to determine the impact of the action(s) that we have carried out. Following on from this, our findings can be reported to other people in the school and even beyond. We can also take informed action on what we will do next.

What are the possibilities for action research in my school?

It may be true to say that the only limitation on the number of possibilities for action research is the boundaries we place on our imagination. The following examples have been investigated in a variety of schools. One or more of these may be appropriate for you and your school, although each school is, of course, unique and will therefore have its own priorities.

- The way in which the words we use as educators can impact on creating a growth mindset.

- Techniques used to change the mindsets of a group of poorly behaved children.

- Raising the self-esteem of students by working with them on mindsets, grit and perseverance.

- Using mindsets to help students welcome challenge.

- Using mindsets to help students see the benefits of failure.

- Using mindset theory to encourage parents to support their children.

- How mindset theory can be used to better motivate staff.

- How mindset theory can be used to better motivate pupils.

- How mindset ideas can help students to become more independent learners.

● How mindsets and AfL (assessment for learning) can combine to great effect to support student learning in maths.

As with all successful actions in a school, action research will work best if at the outset there is a clear vision, focused goals, support from the leadership in the school, a well-structured plan and an enabling culture.

In Part IV we will be looking at practical activities that can be used to train and enthuse both adults and students in the school.

Part IV

Practical activities that change mindsets

Chapter 10
Great activities with pupils

One of the wonderful things about activities designed to help students develop a growth mindset is that we can use our imagination to continuously think of fresh ideas that will invigorate their learning. The following exercises are examples of activities I have developed and used in schools, but they are in no way exhaustive. They might, however, act as a catalyst for your own ideas, and I am sure that you will find many different ways of using and building on these activities which will make them ever more personal and powerful within your own school.

I find that because my RAS is fully primed to be on the lookout for information concerning mindsets, I am constantly discovering new examples of mindset activities that can be used in schools. The activities described here can be used in a range of ways in lessons or assemblies to provide students with a consistent message about the importance of understanding the incredible organ that we call our brain and the way in which we can control a lot of the activity within it, which will then determine our level of success in a variety of pursuits and in our life in general. You can rename and adapt the following activities in any way you wish.

Pupil activity 1: How big is my brain?

This activity really does surprise many people. When I ask teachers and other adults the following question the answers I get vary enormously. So let me ask you the question I ask them: how big is your brain, and how much does your brain weigh?

What did you say? Well, you may recall the answer to this question from Chapter 5, but I have had responses which vary from half a pound up to 20 pounds. The reality is that a baby is born with a brain which is just under 1 pound in weight (around 350–400 g) and an adult has a brain of around 3 pounds.

A great way of demonstrating this weight to both adults and children so that they can get a true feel for what this actually means is to take a freezer bag and pour 16 fluid ounces of water into it (which is the equivalent of 1 pound in weight). If you then tie the top of the freezer bag you can pass around the 'baby's brain'. In another plastic bag you can pour three times this quantity of water and again tie the top of the bag before passing it around. In general, people are very surprised by how heavy both the 'baby brain' and the 'adult brain' feel.

I then usually add comments like: 'It's not the size of your brain that matters but rather what you do with it that counts.' Holding up the 3 pound bag, you can explain that in their brains they have cells (neurons) that are constantly making connections with each other and that there are around 86 billion of these. Each neuron is trying to make connections with other neurons and the connections represent new learning. The more we go over and thoroughly learn something, the stronger the connections become. Each neuron can make up to 10,000 connections with other neurons. (If you were to count each individual neuron in a person's brain and it took one second to count each one, then in total it would take you over 3,000 years to count all of the neurons!)

My aim with this activity is to enable the children (or adults) to gain an appreciation of how magnificent our brains are. This is why we can tell any child with complete sincerity that we don't know and they don't know what they are able to achieve, but what we do know is that the capacity of the brain is immense. History is littered with examples of people who were thought to have very little intelligence when they were young but proved later on in their lives that this was not the case (Einstein and Edison are examples). There are also numerous cases of people who had enormous setbacks early on in their lives but, through perseverance and determination, achieved great ultimate success in their careers (J. K. Rowling and Oprah Winfrey are examples). They learned how to use their brains in a way that released more of their potential. This is something we can all try to do, and where we might eventually get to is part of the magical and unknowable nature of life. We know that IQ can go up or down or stay the same as we get older; the direction it takes is largely determined by the way in which we utilise the capacity of our amazing brains.

SCIENCE REPORT   Summer HALF, 1949.

NAME   GURDON   Division D22   Subject Biology.

Place $\frac{K}{15}$ $\frac{17}{18}$ $\frac{15}{18}$ Marks $\frac{231}{550}$

It has been a disastrous half. His work has been far from satisfactory.
His prepared stuff has been badly learnt, and several of his test pieces
have been torn over; one of such pieces of prepared work scored 2 marks
out of a possible 50. His other work has been equally bad, and several
times he has been in trouble, because he will not listen, but will insist
on doing his work in his own way. I believe he has ideas about becoming
a Scientist; on his present showing this is quite ridiculous, if he can't
learn simple Biological facts he would have no chance of doing the work
of a Specialist, and it would be sheer waste of time, both on his part,
and of those who have to teach him.

Reproduced with the kind permission of The Gurdon Institute.

To say the least the report that John Gurdon received from his school in 1949 was not highly encouraging, particularly as it appeared that he had 'ideas about becoming a scientist'. Fortunately, for us and for John, he did not allow himself to be held back by this early feedback. And, as a result, in 2012 John received the Nobel Prize for Physiology or Medicine for the discovery that mature cells can be converted to stem cells. Professor Sir John Gurdon is a great example of someone who has not allowed early feedback to drive him into developing a fixed and limiting mindset about himself.

Pupil activity 2: What do I store in my brain?

In this activity you might either give the students an A4 or A3 sheet of paper with a simple brain outline drawn on it (as shown below), or you might ask them to draw an outline of a brain themselves.

The idea then is for them to think about all the various things that might be stored in their brain and to write these down inside their brain shape. They may initially think of specific examples of knowledge they have acquired, so they may write down things like maths, science, music, sports and so on. They might then go on to think about the skills they have learned such as how to ride a bike, how to tie a shoelace, how to walk, how to speak or how to use a knife and fork. After this they might start to think about the things that are stored in their brains like the beliefs they have. Some beliefs like Santa Claus may change as we get older and some beliefs we carry with us for the whole of our lives. You might also ask them to write down a number of their beliefs. They might then go on to add other things that are stored in their brains like fears, habits, attitudes, values and expectations.

The aim is that they go on a journey from thinking initially that the brain largely stores facts and information, to a deeper understanding that in fact the brain stores everything about the way we think we are. And all of this is formed from the connections between the neurons in our brain. If we think about beliefs for a moment, then we can understand why it is that once we have a belief it can be hard to change because powerful connections between neurons in our brain have been established. It is not impossible to change the beliefs we hold, but it might take time and effort. The connections in our brain can't be broken, but we can create other connections which start to counterbalance those that have been previously formed (as shown in the diagram below).

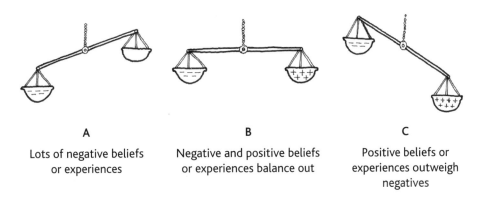

A	B	C
Lots of negative beliefs or experiences	Negative and positive beliefs or experiences balance out	Positive beliefs or experiences outweigh negatives

To take an example, suppose that we believe that we are not good at speaking in front of a number of other people (this is one of the most common fears that people have). Remember, the more we think this and the more we tell ourselves this, the stronger the connections become and so the more powerful this belief becomes. This means that when we stand up in front of people and speak, our belief will make us behave as if we are not good at doing this. You can introduce your students to the TEA-R model here that we looked at in Chapter 7. The thoughts will, of course, come from our beliefs, so if we want to change our thoughts then we may have to change our beliefs.

If you've had a belief for a number of years, then it is hard to just tell your brain to forget it and accept another belief. So what can we do to resolve this dilemma? One possibility is that we can look for positive experiences of talking in front of other people, and when we rehearse these experiences they will begin to be stored in our brains and offset our original belief. This might be difficult because our belief that we are not good at talking in front of people tends to hold us back from achieving the success we desire, so another way is to visualise the success we want to achieve. The more we visualise this and make it as vivid in our minds as possible, the more we will create positive connections in our brain that are going to support us in the future when we do talk in front of people. Athletes and sports people do this all the time with great success (with the exception of the English football team who are so bad at taking penalties that I have the suspicion that they must all have powerfully visualised missing a penalty before they take one!).

This exercise enables students to begin to understand how their thoughts genuinely affect the way they believe they are and how they have a lot of control over who they are and who they want to be. This can be a truly liberating idea for many of them. They have a choice about the person they would like to be, how they would like to see themselves and how they would like other people to see them. This is a metacognitive tool that can serve them well for the rest of their lives, and it applies to what we are referring to here as their mindset. The more they tell themselves that they cannot do something in school (such as maths), the more they will in fact reinforce this with their actions. Therefore they have to be very careful about what they tell themselves. We can add here that studies with many children in many schools show clearly that the mindset they have strongly influences how well they do at school academically. A growth mindset which tells them that with perseverance and deliberate practice they have a very good chance of achieving success is a far better belief for them to have than a fixed mindset which says that they are the way they are and there is not a lot they can do to change this.

Pupil activity 3: If I was a neuron!

This activity is a useful one to do in an assembly, particularly with younger children. It is very simple and the aim of it is to emphasise that the neurons in our brain create connections between each other which represents the learning. I often say to the children that neurons are very sociable characters and they really love to connect with other neurons.

If there are 200 or 300 pupils in a hall, for example, then you can get them to hold hands so that each person is holding hands with two other people. If a child has more than two people holding one of their hands then this is not a problem. A little maths problem you might ask them here is to guess how many connections there are between them. (Answer: there are as many connections between them as there are pupils, so 200 pupils will create 200 connections. To help them understand this you might start by drawing five pupils on a flipchart sheet and demonstrate that their hands would make five connections, then ten pupils would make ten connections and so on.) However, the key thing here is that you have encouraged them to make a guess and it is the guessing that is important and not necessarily getting the right answer – in other words, we are focusing on trying and emphasising that this is crucial if they are going to learn.

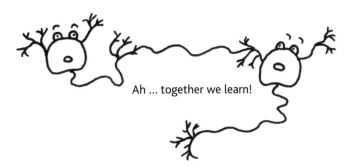

Then you can tell them that there are around seven billion people on earth, and ask, 'If all the people made connections by holding hands with each other, how many connections would there be?' They are now likely to say seven billion, and they would be correct.

However, suppose we have another rule: rather than making connections with other people by holding hands, they have to make a connection by touching their hand onto the feet of two other people and these people must not include anyone who has made a connection with them by touching their feet. If you are brave you might let them have a go at doing this – it could end up as quite a mess but perhaps a fun mess! When you have got them settled again you might ask them to guess how many connections there would be between all the pupils in the hall if they had all managed to be successful in the exercise. Again, it is the encouragement we give them to guess the correct answer rather than praising the correct answer itself that is important. However, if we explore with somebody who has got the right answer how they achieved it, and we focus on the strategy they employed, then this is something that we might decide to give positive feedback about. (Answer: there will be twice as many connections between them as there are pupils in the hall, so 200 pupils will create 400 connections.)

Now let's suppose that each of them had between 1,000 and 10,000 arms and 1,000 and 10,000 feet and there weren't just 200 of them but 86 billion pupils.[1] This is a bit like what we have in our brains. Each neuron can make up to 10,000 connections with other neurons. The total number of connections we can make in our brain is phenomenal. (For the enthusiast: the neurons have 'arms' called axons and 'feet' called dendrites.)

---

1   See R. D. Fields, Brain wiring, *Psychology Today* (21 June 2011). Available at: https://www.psychologytoday.com/blog/the-new-brain/201106/brain-wiring.

Remember that all activities like this are helping the pupils to appreciate how the brain works, and this understanding, as Carol Dweck has shown, encourages them to adopt more of a growth mindset.

Pupil activity 4: Connections make me smarter

This activity complements and builds on activity 3. For this you will need one or more balls of string. It is a good exercise to carry out either at the beginning or end of a lesson. The ball of string is given to one of the students and they are asked to say one thing that they have learned in the lesson or the previous lesson. Then they are asked to pass or throw the ball of string to another student while keeping hold of the loose end. The next student then describes what they have learned in the lesson before they also pass the ball of string on to another student while again holding on to the string. This can continue around the room until all the students have had a chance to contribute something that they have learned or the number of things learned has been exhausted. If a student has already given a contribution but has another one to offer then the ball of string can be passed back to them. Further balls of string can be incorporated into the exercise if needed. The idea is that at the end of the exercise a rich and complex web of string connections has been created between the students in the class, and this is an analogy of the rich learning that has taken place in their brains with neurons making connections with each other.

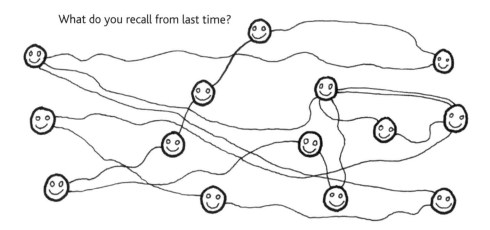

You might also ask the students if there are any learning connections that are not as strong as they would like them to be. If there are then other students could help out with explanations to help the student understand this particular aspect of the learning in a deeper way, providing stronger connections between the neurons for the whole class.

Another variation is to ask the students to give an example of something that they found difficult to learn. Once again the ball of string is passed from student to student with each of them describing things that they have struggled with. You might think that these connections are at present fairly weak, but they provide a great source of further learning. You might ask the students in the class if they can contribute any explanations themselves that will strengthen the learning connections, and if need be you can contribute further knowledge and explanations yourself. This exercise is great for emphasising how important it is to reflect on what we have learned, what we still need to focus more attention on and the importance of asking questions all of the time in order to enhance our learning.

Pupil activity 5: Who hasn't failed before?

When children are very young they are prepared to try so many things that the idea of failure will not hold them back. However, as they get older many children start to fear failure itself, and actively avoid activities at which they think they will not be successful. In their minds they begin to think that if they get something wrong it will make them look silly. Teachers see that this can begin to happen in children at a very early age, and it is part of the fixed mindset mentality which, as educators, we should be trying to direct children away from. But many adults also suffer from this problem. I witness it all the time on the mindset training I provide. To give an example of this, let's go back for a moment to activity 1, where I ask teachers, support staff and other adults to guess the size of an adult brain. Many will be reluctant to give an answer in case they make themselves look stupid in front of their peers. Adlerian psychology (touched on in Chapter 8) informs us that one of the reasons why children and adults may misbehave is because they want to avoid failure. None of us really wants to look stupid or inadequate in front of other people because it impacts negatively on our self-esteem and self-image.

But, of course, failure is an essential part of learning. We learn far more from our failures than from our successes, as long as we can take on board the lessons that failure provide. And therefore we need to constantly emphasise to children that failure is not a dirty word but rather something that we can treat as a precious commodity. Imagine how wonderful it would be if every time a child was unsuccessful at something they adopted a positive attitude and asked themselves, 'What can I learn from this?' and 'How can I do this differently and better next time?' We need to celebrate the magnificence of failure, which may be a tough message to give both to ourselves and to the students. The ultimate aim is for students to be successful and achieve great things for themselves and others. But the key message is that no great achievements ever came about without a lot of trial and error, perseverance, many failures, hard work and dedication.

It is a good idea to give the pupils examples of famous people, and maybe some local people who are not so well known, who achieved great success in a range of ways after failures in their lives. This can be coupled with negative feedback from other people who made unhelpful and patently wrong judgements about them.

In this activity I often display a series of comments about an individual on a PowerPoint slide and ask the children to guess who this person might be. I show the comments or clues as bullet points one at a time. Here are some examples.

Example 1:

- He was slow in learning to talk and was initially thought of as 'backward'.

- His school report said: 'You will never amount to very much.'

- He was asked to leave school at 15 for being 'disruptive' in class.

- He failed to get into the polytechnic school in Zurich to study electronics.

- He failed to get a job as a teacher.

- He later became professor of physics and won the Nobel Prize in Physics.

(Answer: Albert Einstein)

Example 2:

- She had a rough and often abusive childhood.

- She had numerous career setbacks.

- She was fired from her job as a television reporter because she was 'unfit for TV'.

- She is one of the most iconic faces on TV as well as one of the richest and most successful women in the world.

(Answer: Oprah Winfrey)

Example 3:

- At age 7 he was thought of as 'a troublesome boy'.

- At age 9 he 'made very little progress in lessons'.

- He became prime minister in 1940.

- He was widely credited with leading Great Britain and her allies to winning the Second World War.

(Answer: Winston Churchill)

Example 4:

Who do you think said these things?

- 'You must learn to fail intelligently. Failing is one of the greatest arts in the world. One fails forward to success.'

- 'I have not failed. I've just found 10,000 ways that won't work.' (reputedly)

- 'There is no substitute for hard work.'

- 'If we did all the things we are capable of, we would literally astound ourselves.'

(Answer: Thomas Edison)

Example 5:

- She was nearly penniless.

- She has suffered from clinical depression.

- She took the entrance exams for Oxford University but failed to get a place.

- She raised a child on her own while completing a teacher training course and writing a novel.

- She depended on state benefits to survive.

- She is now one of the most successful authors and richest women in the world.

(Answer: J. K. Rowling)

Example 6:

- She faced the failure of rejection multiple times.

- She wrote 15 letters to literary agencies and received 14 rejections. Luckily, one literary agent took her on.

- She has now published a wildly successful series.

(Answer: Stephenie Meyer, author of the 'Twilight' series)

Because your RAS has been ignited you will now be on the lookout to find many more examples of famous people who have struggled against adversity but eventually found their own personal forms of success.

Pupil activity 6: Who is this?

In this exercise the pupils are given a set of statements made by famous people and they have to match these with the correct photograph. I normally produce these using PowerPoint and then print them off with two slides per A4 sheet. Each of the statements reflects a growth mindset approach which has led to the success experienced by each of the individuals. This once again demonstrates that successful people tend to focus on how effort, determination, learning from failure, grit and resilience have been determining factors in what they have achieved in their lives.

An example would be the following:

> The kids look up to me and ask me loads of questions about how I did it. I tell them that I am sure they can do it but it takes time and determination. Boxing doesn't have to be a gift.[2]

The photograph to match this comment would be one of Amir Khan. I usually include a brief piece of information about the person beside the photograph. So here I might write:

> Amir Khan is a British professional boxer and two-time former world champion, having held the unified World Boxing Association and International Boxing Federation light-welterweight titles.

There are further 'Who is this?' examples in Appendix D.

The second part of this activity can be a lot of fun. I ask the pupils to create their own growth mindset statement with their name below it. Some teachers then display these on the classroom wall and refer to them periodically during lessons. I have found that in many instances the children produce statements that can be equally as profound as those spoken by famous people and celebrities. Here are some examples:

> Layali: My brain is my friend and I know if I use it well I can achieve some great things.
>
> John: When I struggle with the work I do I know that I am learning things that will help me in the long term.
>
> Samantha: If I make a mistake it really isn't a problem. I know that I learn all the time by trying, and failure is just a momentary thing that will enable me to think what else I need to do to get to where I want to be.

It can be helpful to give the students a number of opportunities to think of new personal mindsets quotes through the initial year of whole-school mindset training and initiatives.

---

2   Quoted in H. Carter and E. Allison, Amir Khan lends punch to rescue campaign for gym that helped him win Olympic silver, *The Guardian* (23 July 2005). Available at: https://www. theguardian.com/uk/2005/jul/23/boxing.sport.

Pupil activity 7: Telling stories

Human beings communicate with each other through the stories that we share. Storytelling is part of the human condition. We have a story about the day we have just had, the past week, the past month, the past year or indeed our whole life so far. Stories are a great way of illustrating to students certain key ideas and they are particularly useful if they contain universal experiences. These are simply events that most, if not all, of us have experienced at some time in our lives. For example, we were all once a baby, we have all experienced the passage of time, most of us will have received a gift from somebody else (e.g. on a birthday), and most of us will have gone to school and have some recollection of the first day or when we moved from junior to senior school. There is a rich collection of other examples that you could draw on. If you can provide mindset stories that relate to your own experience or the children you have taught (as long as you are not betraying any confidentialities) then the stories tend to work particularly well. However, it is also useful to bring in stories from the broader world which illustrate interesting points about mindsets.

The following example illustrates how the mindset that an individual has impacts on their ability to successfully approach a problem. This is the famous story of George Dantzig (1914–2005). During the time he was a graduate student at the University of California at Berkeley he happened to arrive late to a class given by Professor Jerzy Neyman. By the time Dantzig arrived at the lesson, Neyman had already written two examples of famously unsolved statistics problems on the blackboard. Dantzig wrote these down in the belief that they were homework problems that had been given to the class, and therefore that they were both solvable. Dantzig did later comment that he found them to be 'a little harder than usual'. However, after a few days he handed in his solutions. Six weeks later, Dantzig received a visit from an excited Professor Neyman. He was bursting to tell Dantzig about the true nature of the problems he had attempted and the amazing news that Dantzig had in fact worked out proofs for two unproved statistical theorems. Dantzig says, 'That was the first inkling I had that there was anything special about them.'

In order to solve the problems it is clear that Dantzig had adopted a growth mindset. In other words, he believed that the problems were solvable and that if he put enough effort into solving them then he had a good chance of success. This enabled him to focus his attention simply on finding the solutions. Ignorance about what others might believe to be the 'truth' can thus be a help to someone endeavouring to achieve a complex task.

You might also refer here to the following quote from Chapter 5 of Lewis Carroll's *Through the Looking-Glass* (1871):

> Alice laughed. 'There's no use trying,' she said: 'one can't believe impossible things.'
>
> 'I daresay you haven't had much practice,' said the Queen. 'When I was your age, I always did it for half-an-hour a day. Why, sometimes I've believed as many as six impossible things before breakfast.'

You can ask the students what their thoughts are about this: what is Alice's mindset like, what sort of mindset does the Queen have and how does Alice's mindset compare with that of George Dantzig? If this can be woven into the topic or theme for a lesson then, of course, it will make it ever more relevant and memorable.

Pupil activity 8: A mindsetometer

Another idea is to display what I have decided to call a mindsetometer (like the one below) in your classroom. Emphasise to students that in all we do and say to ourselves and others, we must try to move the dial on the mindsetometer towards the right-hand side. You can use this in a relatively light-hearted way to get over the serious point being made. It is also useful to point out that none of us have a fixed mindset or growth mindset about everything, so we have the choice to shift our mindset when we know that a growth mindset will help us with our school studies and in life in general. It is good to once again refer to the LOC so that this concept becomes firmly understood.

You might ask the students at the beginning (and end) of the lesson where their mindset might be on the mindsetometer today. You can also ask them how much you think this might have affected their learning. There are numerous possibilities for opening up discussions about mindsets through the mindsetometer.

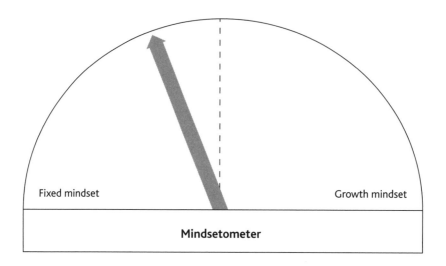

Fixed mindset   Growth mindset

Mindsetometer

Pupil activity 9: Give students a way of developing an understanding of their own learning

A simple way of doing this is:

1. Giving students the opportunity to assess their own work against criteria, model answers or mark schemes.

2. Giving students the opportunity to assess the work of their peers against criteria, model answers or mark schemes.

3. Giving students the opportunity to assess anonymous pieces of work done by students in a previous year against criteria, model answers or mark schemes.

The more that they are able to understand what they are trying to achieve, the more they will be able to take control and move towards mastery of their own learning, and this will encourage them to have a growth mindset. Carol Dweck describes the hallmark of successful individuals as being that 'they love learning, they value effort and they persist in the face of obstacles.'[3] These three activities also encompass assessment for learning.

Pupil activity 10: Chunking for meaning

This activity enables students to look at a topic, thought or idea from different levels (often called logic levels) of perspective. At the higher levels they will be looking at things in a very broad 'big picture' way. As they go further down they will be entering into more and more of the fine detail. As a student gets to understand more about the process of chunking, it will help them to think more about their thinking – in other words, their metacognition. It is also an excellent way of enabling them to structure their ideas when, for example, they are writing an essay in English.

To explain the process, I like to take students on a visualisation exercise where they imagine that they are sitting in a helicopter that takes off from somewhere near to their house, such as their back garden. As the helicopter is about to take off, ask them to look out of the window and describe what they see. Their responses will vary but will include things like the house windows, door, flowers in the garden, greenhouse, perhaps one or two of their family members waving goodbye and so on. As the helicopter gets up to around 100 metres, ask them again to say what they observe. They may refer to things like the road they live on, the houses along the road, perhaps a field nearby, cars travelling along roads, shops in the distance and so on. As they rise to 1,000 metres, ask them once again to look out of the window and describe what they see. They then go even higher still to 10,000 metres and imagine what they might see out of the window. Tell them that this helicopter is a very special one and it is able to ascend up

---

3   C. S. Dweck, *Self-Theories: Their Role in Motivation, Personality, and Development* (1st edn) (Philadelphia, PA: Psychology Press, 1999), p. 1.

into the earth's outer atmosphere (assure them that they will have the necessary breathing apparatus to enable them to survive!). As they rise, some students will say that they can start to see the outline of England and Britain, then Europe, Africa and so on. They may even take themselves high enough to be able to see the curvature of the planet.

Then ask them to very gently bring themselves back down to earth, once again observing what they see as they descend back into their garden. When they have landed, ask them to step out of the helicopter and walk through the door of their house. Ask them to say what they see now. They then walk into the kitchen and go to the fridge, open the fridge door and again describe what they see. They take out something to eat or drink and sit down in their favourite place to enjoy this. As they look at their food or drink ask them to describe this in as much detail as possible.

You have just taken them through a 'chunking' experience, where every level has allowed them to see things differently. In a similar way, we can explain how it is possible to ask ourselves certain simple questions in order to alter our thinking between big picture and fine detail perspectives. We can also use questions that help us to move across laterally at the same level of thinking to enable us to look at things that are similar to what we are considering. Let's see how this works.

Questions that allow us to move up to a higher, bigger picture level include the following:

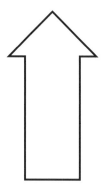

- What is this (or that) an example of?

- What is the purpose of this?

- What is the intention of this?

- What does this do for you?

- What is this part of?

- What is important about this?

- What will this do for you?

Questions that allow us to move down into the finer detail include the following:

- What is a detail of this?

- What is a component of this?

- Tell me exactly how you do this.

- What is a part of this?

- What is an example of this?

- Give me a specific instance of this.

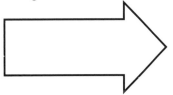

And questions that take us laterally include the following:

- What else would be in the same category?

- What else does something similar to this?

- What are other examples of this?

Now let us take a couple of examples to illustrate how these questions might work and where they might take us in terms of our thinking. One example might be 'using mindsets in classrooms' and another might be 'seatbelts in cars'. It is important to realise that different people will give different responses to the chunking questions, although there are often a lot of similarities too – as we go to the very highest levels, in particular, we will generally find a sense of agreement and convergence on our individual thoughts. In fact, this is why when we are arguing a particular point, it is often useful to start at a high logic level so that we can create agreement with the people around us at the outset. The number of logic levels that we go up or down, or the number of steps we take laterally, is up to us.

For the first example of 'using mindsets in classrooms' you might want to imagine that you are about to explain to the staff in your school why you believe this is important, and you want to use the chunking procedure to develop your thoughts and arguments before the meeting. By using the chunking questions given above, you might end up with something that looks like this the flow chart on the following pages.

Practical activities that change mindsets

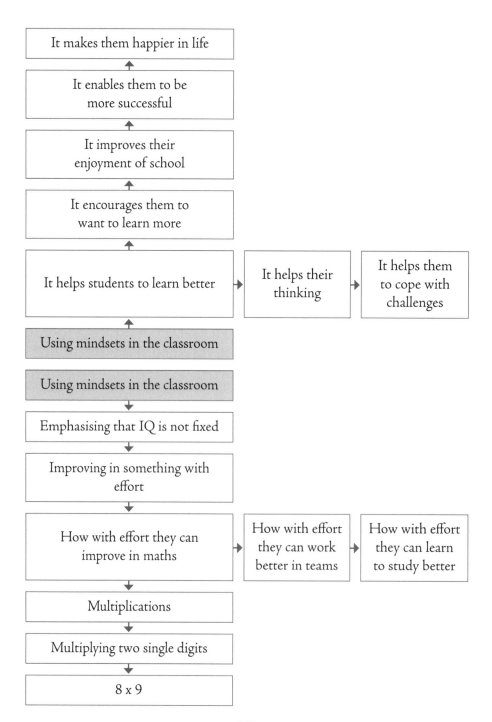

Now let's consider the topic of 'seatbelts in cars'.

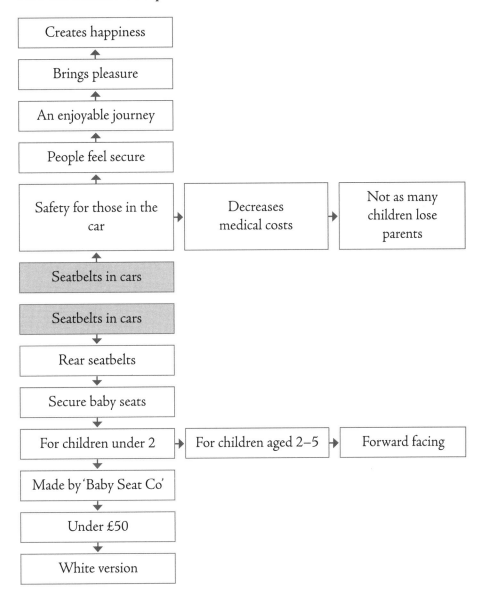

By teaching children about chunking and logic levels we can help them to think more clearly, to understand their thinking better, to organise their ideas and to learn better. The chunking process enables children to take greater control of their learning, and this increased autonomy supports them to move to higher levels of mastery.

A chunking (or logic levels) structure plan which the students can use might look something like the one below. This takes the student from high level, big picture thinking down into progressively finer detail.

Main topic:								
Major area 1			Major area 2			Major area 3		
Key point 1a	Key point 1b	Key point 1c	Key point 2a	Key point 2b	Key point 2c	Key point 3a	Key point 3b	Key point 3c

Chunking allows a student to thoroughly analyse, understand and complete a task while at the same time helping them to organise their learning.

Chapter 11
Great adult activities – training with teachers, support staff and parents

I have decided to gather together the training activities for teachers, support staff and parents as there is a great deal of crossover in most cases. You can choose which of these activities you use with the different groups.

Adult activity 1: The seven day diet

I created this activity to be used mainly with parents, but it can be adapted as a reminder of the key messages that all members of the school can give to children. I call this 'The seven day diet' and it can be given as a takeaway (forgive the pun!) at the end of a mindset parents' evening. Since many people are often on a diet (or in my case thinking about going on a diet), I thought it would be topical to introduce the notion of a mindset diet. This is something that each parent can focus on over the course of a week with different mindset messages being 'fed' to their children each day. Then the diet of seven days of messages can begin once more. The full seven day diet that I have used is given in Appendix E but a typical day of mindset messages could include:

Monday. Failure, challenge and risks day:

- Emphasising to my son/daughter that we all learn from failure.
- Giving examples of how I have learned from failures.
- Encouraging my son/daughter to take on a new challenge.
- Encouraging my son/daughter to take risks.

You might, of course, decide on a very different set of messages for parents to deliver to their children depending on what you believe the key priorities to be in your school. The main purpose of this exercise is to involve parents in something that they can take active control over. Some parents might decide on certain messages that they believe to be important, and if they can feed these back to the school then an interesting dialogue can result with mutual learning taking place.

Adult activity 2: A diamond nine of mindset messages

I have used this activity with teachers and school support staff, and it can be used with parents as well. The idea of a diamond nine is to prioritise a set of statements – usually there are ten of them. It is best done in groups of three or four people so they can discuss what they each consider to be the most important statements. This reflection and discussion is very important. The following set of ten statements might be used for this exercise, but equally you could make up your own.

1. Intelligence is not fixed. This is scientifically proven along with the fact that education increases IQ and that we all learn at different rates and in different ways.

2. The 'truth' that many of the most successful and creative people were once judged to have low intelligence.

3. What you are able to achieve nobody knows.

4. What you will achieve will be mostly down to your effort.

5. To learn requires effort. Remind children that if the work is not hard, they are not learning (this helps them to accept high challenge).

6. When you learn, connections in your brain are created that makes it more efficient at learning more – you become smarter.

7. Great learners learn by asking questions – they seek support.

8. Great learners make mistakes. This is how we learn.

9. Be careful what you tell yourself.

10. Be careful what other people tell you.

Each of the statements can be printed onto pieces of paper so that the groups can move them around as they discuss the order of importance. The idea is that each group makes up a diamond nine pattern as shown below.

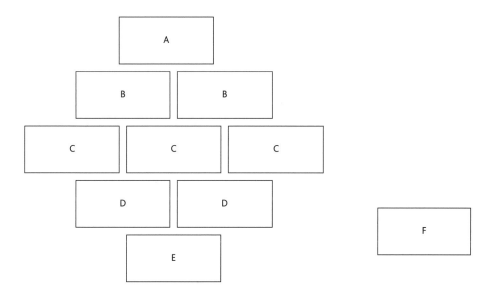

A, at the top of the diamond nine, is the statement that the group believes to be the most important mindset message to deliver to the students at the present time. The B statements are what the group believes are the next two most important statements, and so on with E being the least important statement, except for F which has been removed. It will not surprise you to hear that there is usually a lot of initial disagreement within groups about the order of importance, and this is exactly what the exercise is meant to encourage. There is no right and wrong answer, but the process of discussing the different messages is the valuable part of this exercise because it will enable people to remember the statements with far greater clarity than if they had simply been given the list. It is also interesting to listen to how the different groups justify the top message that each of them has decided on, which can create even more of a heated debate.

I generally ask each person to take their top three messages and create three affirmations about these that will help them to reinforce these with the students over a period of one or two weeks. They might then decide to take on further messages, for which they also write affirmations, and focus on these for another one or two weeks. This is all part of the drip feed that will sustain a constant growth mindset culture throughout the school.

Adult activity 3: The language we use

However careful we might be as educators in the language we use with children, there may be times when we say things that do not deliver the results we are looking for. This goes back to the unintended consequences of our actions. As the things we say can have such a significant impact, it is important that everyone in the school considers the language that is used in a range of different situations.

In this exercise I generally like to ask staff to work in groups of three or four. Each small group is then given a scenario and asked to think about the language they would use with their students. The small groups are then asked to report back to the whole group about what they decided to say to the students and their reasoning behind this. The whole group can then give their views and offer any suggestions that they believe would make what is said to the students even more effective.

Here is an example of a scenario: Suppose you have a student who has improved their results in maths and you are aware that they have changed the way they have studied. What might you say? One possibility is: 'You clearly studied well for your maths test and the improvement in your results really shows this.' The focus is on the studying and how this has led to an improvement in the results for the student. This kind of response encourages and supports the development of a growth mindset approach by the student.

The exercise can be extended further by asking the groups to consider other interesting scenarios they have either encountered or can imagine and to write these on sheets of paper. These scenarios are then passed on to other groups, but before doing this each group is also asked to decide on the response that they might give to their own scenario and write it on another piece of paper which they keep to themselves. Each of the groups is then asked to consider what they would say in the scenarios they have been given before they all report back to the whole group. Debate can then take place between the group that created the scenario and the group that considered it. The whole group can contribute as well.

This activity helps all of us as educators to become more consciously aware of what we say and how we might try to make what we say even more effective. It enables us to be, in the first instance, consciously competent about the things we say in order that this can be locked into our brains through the connections between our neurons. This means that we can then begin to operate in an unconsciously competent way which will hopefully deliver the results we are looking for. As highly competent professionals we must, on a regular basis, be reflective (i.e. operate as reflective practitioners at a reflectively competent level) about the things we are saying so that we do not lapse into a state of complacency where we slip back into saying things that are not having the effect that we desire. Further scenarios that you can use for this exercise can be found in Appendix F.

Adult activity 4: How to praise

This activity follows on from the one above and focuses specifically on the kind of praise that can have a positive impact on the students' learning. Research has shown that praise and other rewards can have the kind of negative unintended consequences that we have considered in this book. The difficulty can be that, as caring adults who want to give children as much positive feedback as we can, we may focus on the wrong things. Praise about the person should be avoided; instead, we should focus on praising learning behaviours.

As educators most of us will have learned a very important message, which is that saying to a child who has misbehaved, 'You are a very naughty child,' is never a good thing to do because it gives the young person an intrinsically negative idea about themselves as an individual. They might then think to themselves, 'Well, if you think I've been naughty so far you ain't seen nothing yet!' However, if we say to them, 'Your behaviour was unacceptable and I don't expect this from you,' then we are clearly focusing on the actions or behaviours of the child and not them as a person. The message also has a positive in it, because the adult is saying that they don't expect this kind of behaviour from the child. The child can very easily, if they want to, decide to change the way they are behaving.

In a similar way, we should always remind ourselves to constantly refer to the actions, methods and techniques that the student is using in order to carry out a learning activity, rather than commenting on the student themselves or, indeed, placing too much focus on the final outcome of their endeavours. It is also important to try to make the comment as specific as possible because this will give the student clarity about the things they are doing well, or not so well, and therefore help them with their future actions.

The activity involves the ten pieces of advice given about positive praise shown below. You could begin this activity by asking the adults to create a diamond nine as we did in adult activity 2. Following on from this you might ask individuals or groups to think of specific words that they might use in classroom situations, or anywhere around the school or at home, associated with one or more of the ten statements of praise and advice. All of this helps us to hardwire into our brains the kinds of praise that will support the learning of our students, both now and in the future.

1. Always focus on the learning actions or behaviour rather than the child themselves.

2. Try giving praise privately to a child.

3. Always talk about their effort and not their intelligence or ability.

4. Point out to them when they have taken on difficult or complex tasks.

5. Don't over praise but give it in a genuine and sincere way.

6. Highlight when they have shown resilience, grit and determination.

7. Talk to them about the effective strategies they have used to help them learn.

8. Be specific in praise rather than using general comments.

9. Talk to them about improvements they have made and how they have managed to do this.

10. Praise specific examples of when a child supports another child with their learning (it helps both children in their learning).

Adult activity 5: Giving feedback on work

This activity builds on activities 3 and 4 above. Professor John Hattie says that there are three levels to giving effective specific feedback to students: these are at the task level, process level and self-regulation level.[1] All of these have benefits, but it may be argued that the self-regulation level is the highest level and can, in the long term, have the greatest impact on the ability of the student to take full control of their own learning. My own interpretation, with examples, of the different levels is given here.

Task level feedback

This feedback covers how well the student is carrying out the task. Comments should be simple and help the student to build their confidence to take the task forward. We might say something like, 'You have given five convincing benefits for wind energy. Can you now think of five reasons why people might not want to have wind farms near their homes?'

Process level feedback

Feedback at the process level has been shown to provide deeper learning than at the task level. It also raises the students' self-efficacy – their belief that they

---

1   Hattie and Timperley, The power of feedback.

themselves can achieve success – which is central to them building a growth mindset. Here we might ask a student coaching questions to help them consider different ways of approaching a task. This supports them in developing strategies that they can use in the long term with other learning tasks. We might also encourage them to look for connections between ideas they have expressed. An important aspect to emphasise and ask them about is the learning they have got from the things they have initially got wrong or that they have found challenging. Here we might say something like, 'You have brainstormed a lot of ideas about Macbeth's character. Would it be useful if you ranked these in order of which played the biggest part in his actions? You could use a diamond nine exercise for this that you will remember we have used before.' Later on you could perhaps add, 'And now, as you look at the diamond nine pattern, is there anything else that you may have missed out that is also an important part of Macbeth's character?'

Self-regulation level feedback

At the self-regulation level we want the student to consider their own strategies for learning. We want them to think about what went well and what might have made their learning even better. This is a deeper level of feedback and learning than at the task or process level. We are encouraging them to self-monitor, self-assess and self-regulate their learning. Self-regulation helps the students to set goals, plan their work, take control of their work and determine how they can move from their present level to the level they are aspiring to achieve. Here we might say something like, 'You know how important punctuation is in terms of enabling a reader to benefit most from what we have written. Can you look over your work and decide where your use of punctuation has been most effective and where you might need to add further punctuation in order to improve this essay even more?'

In fact, Hattie goes on to talk about a fourth level of feedback which is called 'the self'. This links with the praise of the individual that we considered above and which can be highly counter-productive. We might say to a student, 'That's brilliant,' 'You've shown me yet again how clever you are' or even, 'What a beautiful picture!' This can actively take the student's focus away from the task, the process and their self-regulation of their learning. Although many students will have grown to expect this sort of praise, it rarely, if ever, helps their learning. It gives them no insight into how they might improve their learning, and when it is mixed with the other three positive feedback categories discussed above it can dilute the impact they have.

To carry out an activity around effective feedback, you might decide to ask individual adults or groups to focus on task, process and self-regulation feedback and to think of real-life examples that fit these three categories. They can write these down on A4 sheets with a marker pen and then, one at a time, they can hold them up, read them out and ask the rest of the group to decide whether the feedback is at the task, process or self-regulation level. My experience is that this can create some great debate which enables people to begin to fully understand these different levels of feedback. Alternatively, you could provide a set of statements which individuals or groups can separate into task, process and self-regulation statements.

Appendices

Appendix A
School focus and goal setting document

The mindset for success programme extends over a whole school year or more. It is important at the outset that any school embarking on the programme has clarity about the main school focus for the intervention. The following is therefore to be used as a means of reflection and goal setting. Try to ensure that goals are SMARTER:

S = Specific

M = Measurable

A = Achievable

R = Realistic

T = Time bound

E = Energising

R = Rewarding

Stage 1	THE OVERALL GOAL

OVERALL GOAL of the mindset for success programme is:

Stage 2	SUB-GOALS

You might have one, two, three or more sub-goals. Each of these should support the overall goal.

FIRST SUB-GOAL of the mindset for success programme is:

SECOND SUB-GOAL of the mindset for success programme is:

THIRD SUB-GOAL of the mindset for success programme is:

FOURTH SUB-GOAL of the mindset for success programme is:

FIFTH SUB-GOAL of the mindset for success programme is:

Stage 3	**THE BENEFITS.** The following are three important benefits for the pupils that will come from successfully achieving the goal and sub-goals. These are benefits of the desired future and not an escape from negative aspects of the current situation.

Appendix A: School focus and goal setting document

BENEFIT 1 is:

BENEFIT 2 is:

BENEFIT 3 is:

Stage 4	**THE BARRIERS.** The following are three barriers that we need to overcome to achieve the overall goal and sub-goals.

BARRIER 1 is:

BARRIER 2 is:

BARRIER 3 is:

Stage 5	**STEPS TO OVERCOME THE BARRIERS.** The following are three steps we will take to overcome the barriers.

STEP 1 is:

STEP 2 is:

STEP 3 is:

Appendix B
Example of a 12 month mindset for success programme

Day	For	Details	Time allocation	Days	Proposed date
1	Teachers, support staff and 'mindset ambassadors' children	Session with the 'mindset ambassadors' children – 9.00–11.00	2 hours	1 day	
		Mindsets 1. Support staff – 1.30–3.30	2 hours		
		Mindsets 1. Teaching staff – 3.45–5.45	2 hours		
2	Pupils, teachers, support staff, 'mindset ambassadors' children and parents	Assembly 1	90 minutes	1 day	
		Interview some of the 'mindset ambassadors' children – 10.30–12.00	90 minutes		
		Mindsets 2. Support staff – 1.30–3.30	2 hours		
		Mindsets 2. Teaching staff – 3.45–5.45	2 hours		
		Parents' evening 1 – 7.00–9.00	2 hours		

A mindset for success

Day	For	Details	Time allocation	Days	Proposed date
3	Teachers, support staff and 'mindset ambassadors' children	Interview some of the 'mindset ambassadors' children – 9.00–11.00	2 hours	1 day	
		Mindsets 3. Support staff – 1.30–3.30	2 hours		
		Mindsets 3. Teaching staff – 3.45–5.45	2 hours		
4	Teachers, support staff and 'mindset ambassadors' children	Interview some of the 'mindset ambassadors' children – 9.00–11.00	2 hours	1 day	
		Mindsets 4. Support staff – 1.30–3.30	2 hours		
		Mindsets 4. Teaching staff – 3.45–5.45	2 hours		
5	Teachers and support staff	Visit classrooms	2 hours	1 day	
		Mindsets 5. Support staff – 1.30–3.30	2 hours		
		Mindsets 5. Teaching staff – 3.45–5.45	2 hours		
6	Pupils, teachers, support staff and parents	Assembly 2	90 minutes	1 day	
		Mindsets 6. Support staff – 1.30–3.30	2 hours		
		Mindsets 6. Teaching staff – 3.45–5.45	2 hours		
		Parents' evening 2 – 7.00–9.00	2 hours		

Appendix B: Example of a 12 month mindset for success programme

Day	For	Details	Time allocation	Days	Proposed date
7	Teachers, support staff and 'mindset ambassadors' children	Interview some of the 'mindset ambassadors' children – 9.00–11.00	2 hours	1 day	
		Mindsets 7. Support staff – 1.30–3.30	2 hours		
		Mindsets 7. Teaching staff – 3.45–5.45	2 hours		
8	Pupils, teachers, support staff and parents	Morning for parents to be invited into the school	2 hours	1 day	
		Mindsets 8. Support staff – 1.30–3.30	2 hours		
		Mindsets 8. Teaching staff – 3.45–5.45	2 hours		
			TOTAL	8 days	

Appendix C
The ABCDE model

Adversity – Write down the adversity (misfortune, bad luck, trouble, difficulty). Include the who, what, when and where of the situation. The more accurate and specific you are the better. Try to be as descriptive as possible (focus on the facts) rather than bringing in your beliefs.

Belief – Describe how you interpret the adversity. This is about your thoughts and not your feelings (your feelings are recorded in the consequence section below). If you say, 'I really think I'm hopeless,' then this is a belief, and if you say, 'I'm never going to be able to do this,' this is also a belief.

Consequence – Record the consequences of your beliefs. This includes the feelings you have and the things you might have done (how you acted and behaved) as a result of those feelings. Again, be very specific and record as many feelings and actions as possible. You also need to ask yourself if the consequences make sense based on your beliefs.

Disputation – Try to find any evidence that brings into doubt your beliefs. Then try to think of other alternative beliefs about the adversity which are more positive and optimistic, or try to reframe your beliefs and put them into perspective in order to make them more accurate and optimistic. Here are some useful phrases to use in the disputation stage to help with your ideas:

a)   Evidence: That's not completely true because ...

b)   Alternative: A more accurate way of seeing this is ...

c)   Putting it in perspective: The most likely outcome of this is ... and I can ... to handle it.

Energisation – The energisation is what you feel and get from redirecting your thoughts and attention. Write down here how the disputation has enabled you to change the energy level you feel, your mood and how you behave. You also might add here any solutions that you now see that you were unable to see before.

Appendix D
Who is this?

The quotes on the left are immediately opposite the respective owners on the right. You can cut these up and mix them up. Students can then work in groups of three to match the quotes with the people who said them.

'You can never guarantee the wins but you can guarantee that you give it 100%. That way you can always look back and feel comfortable, as a player or coach.'[1]	Ivan Lendl is from the Czech Republic and became the world number one professional tennis player. He was dominant in the 1980s and maintained a high position in the men's game until the early 1990s. Later on he coached Andy Murray.
'I believe that you can always get better. It's the mindset I always try to have because it's something that keeps me going every single day on the practice courts. There is still room for improvement. That's something that excites me for the future.'[2]	Novak Djokovic is from Serbia and became the number one men's singles tennis player in the world. He held on to the Association of Tennis Professionals number one spot for over four years before being overtaken by Andy Murray in 2016.
'Anyone who has never made a mistake has never tried anything new.' (commonly attributed to)	Albert Einstein was born in Germany and is most famous for his general theory of relativity which revolutionised the way that we think about space and time.

....

1 Quoted in K. Mitchell, Ivan Lendl enjoys the crack as unlikely double act take centre stage, *The Guardian* (13 January 2012). Available at: https://www.theguardian.com/sport/2012/jan/13/ivan-lendl-andy-murray-australian-open.

2 Quoted in *Evening Standard*, Novak Djokovic always believes he will win but Andy Murray only thinks he can (5 July 2013). Available at: http://www.standard.co.uk/sport/sport-comment/novak-djokovic-always-believes-he-will-win-but-andy-murray-only-thinks-he-can-8688534.html.

'I don't think limits.' (commonly attributed to)	Usain Bolt was born in Jamaica and presently holds the 100 and 200 metre world records.
'I attribute my success to this – I never gave or took any excuse.'[3]	Florence Nightingale rose to fame during the Crimean War, when she served as a manager and trainer of nurses who tended to wounded soldiers.
'Winners never quit, and quitters never win.'[4]	Dame Kelly Holmes won gold medals in the 800 and 1500 metres events in the 2004 Summer Olympics in Athens.

. . . .

3   Quoted in A. Anderson, Profiles in greatness: Florence Nightingale, *SUCCESS*.com (5 April 2010). Available at: http://www.success.com/article/profiles-in-greatness-florence-nightingale.

4   Quoted in BBC, Star in the making, *BBC Sport* (11 April 2006). Available at: http://news.bbc.co.uk/sport1/hi/athletics/get_involved/4897456.stm.

Appendix E
The seven day diet

The seven day parenting plan for building growth mindsets

Take one a day for seven days!

This seven day diet is described in more detail in Chapter 11. The idea is that the following programme (or something similar) can be given to parents so they can work with their children on a uniform message about important aspects of growth mindsets. Although it is presented as a seven day programme, parents can use this in whatever way they feel is most appropriate. It is important that parents realise that the messages should be revisited on a regular basis and in different ways. This then complements the work that the school itself will be doing on mindsets.

1. Informing them that IQ is not fixed.

2. Emphasising that we learn from failure.

3. Focusing on effort and perseverance.

4. Focusing on actions.

5. Encouraging reasonable risk taking.

6. Giving honest feedback.

7. Being a role model.

Day 1: Informing them that IQ is not fixed

You might tell your child:

- The first IQ test was devised by the French psychologist Alfred Binet, but he never meant for IQ to be thought of as fixed.

- It is scientifically proven that IQ is not fixed: education increases IQ.

- We all learn at different rates and in different ways.

- The 'truth' that many of the most successful and creative people were once judged to have low intelligence.

- What you are able to achieve nobody knows.

Day 2: Emphasising that we learn from failure

Things to consider discussing with your child:

- Encouraging reasonable risks.

- That great learners make mistakes – this is how they learn.

- Not placing any blame for failure on others.

- When they fail, ask them: 'What can you learn from this experience? What could you try differently the next time?'

Day 3: Focusing on effort and perseverance

You might tell your child:

- What they will achieve will be mostly down to their effort.

- To learn requires effort.

- If the work is not hard, then they are not learning (this helps them to accept high challenge).

- Great learners learn by asking questions – they seek support.

- When your child succeeds, talk about the work that went into the success.

- Praise persistence and perseverance. Focus on the positive habits your child practised and the choices she/he made which led to the success.

Day 4: Focusing on actions

Think about:

- Not labelling them (e.g. as good or bad, as intelligent or otherwise).

- Identify actions that they might take.

- Point out good things they do.

Day 5: Encouraging reasonable risk taking

Encourage your child to:

- Try new things.

- Step out of their comfort zone (with support).

- Enjoy the fun in doing something new.

Day 6: Giving honest feedback

You should:

- Never tell them untruths.

- Never tell them they have done something that is great if it is not.

- Give specific rather than general feedback.

- Help them with finding the next step.

Day 7: Being a role model

You might:

- Tell them that you are a lifelong learner.

- Tell them what you learned from a failure in your life.

- Tell them about something that you are going to try and have been afraid to do before.

Appendix F
The language we use

The 'what you might say' suggestions are simply given as possibilities. You may well think of many other things that you might say to encourage your students to adopt a growth mindset.

Scenario	What you might say
You have a child who has done a good piece of work in class.	'You read the material over several times, you picked out the main points and you tested yourself on them. It really worked!'
You want to give positive feedback on the way a child has used a range of strategies to complete a piece of work.	'I like the way you tried all kinds of strategies on that maths problem until you finally got it.'
You want to encourage a child to not give up.	'Everyone learns in a different way. Let's keep trying to find the way that works for you.'
You want to give the message that struggling with work is part of learning.	'Who had a good struggle? Let's share what we struggled with today.'
A child used to find certain work somewhat easy but now they are struggling. How can you turn this into a positive?	'I know school used to be easy for you and you used to feel like the smart kid all the time. But the truth is that you weren't using your brain to the fullest. I'm really excited about how you're stretching yourself now and working to learn hard things.'

Bibliography

Allen, J. (1902) *As a Man Thinketh*. Available at: http://gutenberg.org/files/4507/4507-h/4507-h.htm.

Anderson, A. (2010). Profiles in greatness: Florence Nightingale, *SUCCESS.com* (5 April). Available at: http://www.success.com/article/profiles-in-greatness-florence-nightingale.

BBC (2006). Star in the making, *BBC Sport* (11 April). Available at: http://news.bbc.co.uk/sport1/hi/athletics/get_involved/4897456.stm.

Binet, A. (1974 [1909]). Les idées modernes sur les enfants, *Population*, 29(3), 664.

Blackwell, L. S., Trzesniewski, K. H. and Dweck, C. S. (2007). Implicit theories of intelligence predict achievement across an adolescent transition: a longitudinal study and an intervention, *Child Development*, 78(1), 246–263 at 251.

Bloom, B. and Sosniak, L. (1985). *Developing Talent in Young People* (New York: Ballantine Books).

Brooks, D. (2012). *The Social Animal: The Hidden Sources of Love, Character, and Achievement* (London: Short Books).

Brooks, E. B. (2001). Tales of statisticians: George B Dantzig, *Umass.edu*. Available at: https://www.umass.edu/wsp/resources/tales/dantzig.html.

CareerTech Testing Center (2010). The sigmoid curve, personal learning, and the 'business' of education (30 November). Available at: http://careertechtesting.blogspot.co.uk/2010/11/sigmoid-curve-personal-learning-and.html.

Carter, H. and Allison, E. (2005). Amir Khan lends punch to rescue campaign for gym that helped him win Olympic silver, *The Guardian* (23 July). Available at: https://www.theguardian.com/uk/2005/jul/23/boxing.sport.

Covey, S. (1989). *The Seven Habits of Highly Effective People: Restoring the Character Ethic* (New York: Free Press).

Coyle, D. (2009). *The Talent Code: Greatness Isn't Born. It's Grown* (New York: Bantam Books).

Cranmer-Byng, L. and Kapadi, S. A. (eds) (1905). *The Sayings of Lao-Tzŭ*, tr. L. Giles (New York: E. P. Dutton).

Dijksterhuis, A. (2004). Think different: the merits of unconscious thought in preference development and decision making, *Journal of Personality and Social Psychology*, 87(5), 586–598.

Dijksterhuis, A. and van Knippenberg, A. (1998). The relation between perception and behavior, or how to win a game of *Trivial Pursuit*, *Journal of Personality and Social Psychology*, 74, 865–877.

Dixon, A. (2002). Editorial, *FORUM*, 44(1), 1.

Duckworth, A. (2013). Grit: the power of passion and perseverance [video], *TED.com* (April). Available at: https://www.ted.com/talks/angela_lee_duckworth_grit_the_power_of_passion_and_perseverance.

Dweck, C. S. (1999). Caution – praise can be dangerous, *American Educator*, 21(1), 4–9.

Dweck, C. S. (1999). *Self-Theories: Their Role in Motivation, Personality, and Development* (1st edn) (Philadelphia, PA: Psychology Press).

Dweck, C. S. (2006). *Mindset: The New Psychology of Success* (New York: Random House).

Elliott, A. and Dweck, C. (2005). *Handbook of Competence and Motivation* (New York: Guilford Press).

Ericsson, K. A., Krampe, R. and Tesch-Romer, C. (1993). The role of deliberate practice in the acquisition of expert performance, *Psychological Review*, 100(3), 363–406.

Evening Standard (2013). Novak Djokovic always believes he will win but Andy Murray only thinks he can (5 July). Available at: http://www.standard.co.uk/sport/sport-comment/novak-djokovic-always-believes-he-will-win-but-andy-murray-only-thinks-he-can-8688534.html.

Fassler, D. and Dumas, L. (1997). *Help Me, I'm Sad* (New York: Viking).

Faurote, F. L. (1928). My philosophy of industry [interview with Henry Ford], *The Forum*, 79(4), 481.

Bibliography

Fields, R. D. (2011). Brain wiring, *Psychology Today* (21 June). Available at: https://www.psychologytoday.com/blog/the-new-brain/201106/brain-wiring.

Fredrickson, B. (1998). What good are positive emotions? *Review of General Psychology*, 2(3), 300–319.

Gaser, C. and Schlaug, G. (2001). Brain structures differ between musicians and non-musicians, *NeuroImage*, 13(6), 1168.

Ginott, H. G. (1972). *Teacher and Child: A Book for Parents and Teachers* (New York: Macmillan).

Gladwell, M. (2005). *Blink: The Power of Thinking Without Thinking* (New York: Little, Brown and Co.).

Gladwell, M. (2008). *Outliers: The Story of Success* (New York: Little, Brown and Co.).

Goleman, D. (2006). *Emotional Intelligence: Why It Can Matter More Than IQ* (New York: Bantam Books).

Goleman, D., Boyatzis, R. and McKee, A. (2002). *Primal Leadership: Unleashing the Power of Emotional Intelligence* (Boston, MA: Harvard Business School Press).

Green, H., McGinnity, A., Meltzer, H., Ford, T. and Goodman, R. (2005). *Mental Health of Children and Young People in Great Britain 2004* (Basingstoke: Palgrave Macmillan).

Haimovitz, K. and Dweck, C. (2016). What predicts children's fixed and growth intelligence mind-sets? Not their parents' views of intelligence but their parents' views of failure, *Psychological Science*, 27(6), 859–869.

Hattie, J. (2009). *Visible Learning* (London: Routledge).

Hattie, J. (2012). *Visible Learning for Teachers* (London: Routledge).

Hattie, J. and Timperley, H. (2007). The power of feedback, *Review of Educational Research*, 77(1), 81–112.

Hattie, J. and Yates, G. (2014). *Visible Learning and the Science of How We Learn* (Abingdon and New York: Routledge).

Hay McBer (2000). *Research into Teacher Effectiveness: A Model of Teacher Effectiveness*. Research report no. 216 (Norwich: DfEE/HMSO). Available at: http://webarchive.nationalarchives.gov.uk/20130401151715/http://www.education.gov.uk/publications/eorderingdownload/rr216.pdf.

Heckman, J. and Masterov, D. (2007). The productivity argument for investing in young children, *Review of Agricultural Economics*, 29(3), 446–493.

Howe, M., Davidson, J. and Sloboda, J. (1998). Innate talents: reality or myth? *Behavioral and Brain Sciences*, 21(3), 399–442.

Isen, A., Daubman, K. and Nowicki, G. (1987). Positive affect facilitates creative problem solving, *Journal of Personality and Social Psychology*, 52(6), 1122–1131.

Isen, A., Rosenzweig, A. and Young, M. (1991). The influence of positive affect on clinical problem solving, *Medical Decision Making*, 11(3), 221–227.

Kahneman, D. (2012). *Thinking, Fast and Slow* (London: Penguin).

Leimon, A., Moscovici, F. and McMahon, G. (2005). *Essential Business Coaching* (1st edn) (London: Routledge).

Lepper, M. P., Greene, D. and Nisbett, R. E. (1973). Undermining children's intrinsic interest with extrinsic reward: a test of the 'overjustification' hypothesis, *Journal of Personality and Social Psychology*, 28(1), 129–137.

Lewinsohn, P., Rohde, P., Seeley, J. and Fischer, S. (1993). Age-cohort changes in the lifetime occurrence of depression and other mental disorders, *Journal of Abnormal Psychology*, 102(1), 110–120.

Lilienfeld, S. (2010). *50 Great Myths of Popular Psychology: Shattering Widespread Misconceptions about Human Behavior* (Chichester: Wiley-Blackwell).

Lyubomirsky, S. (2007). *The How of Happiness: A New Approach to Getting the Life You Want* (New York: Penguin).

Lyubomirsky, S., Sheldon, K. and Schkade, D. (2005). Pursuing happiness: the architecture of sustainable change, *Review of General Psychology*, 9(2), 111–131.

Maguire, E., Woollett, K. and Spiers, H. (2006). London taxi drivers and bus drivers: a structural MRI and neuropsychological analysis, *Hippocampus*, 16(12), 1091–1101.

Bibliography

Mansell, W. (2008). Research reveals teaching's Holy Grail, *TES* (21 November). Available at: https://www.tes.com/news/tes-archive/tes-publication/research-reveals-teachings-holy-grail.

Maslow, A. (1943). A theory of human motivation, *Psychological Review*, 50(4), 370–396.

Mechelli, A., Crinion, J., Noppeney, U., O'Doherty, J., Ashburner, J., Frackowiak, R. and Price, C. (2004). Neurolinguistics: structural plasticity in the bilingual brain, *Nature*, 431(7010), 757.

Mehrabian, A. (1981). *Silent Messages: Implicit Communication of Emotions and Attitudes* (Belmont, CA: Wadsworth).

Michalko, M. (2006). *Thinkertoys: A Handbook of Creative-Thinking Techniques* (Berkeley, CA: Ten Speed Press).

Michelon, P. (2008). Brain plasticity: how learning changes your brain, *SharpBrains* (26 February). Available at: http://sharpbrains.com/blog/2008/02/26/brain-plasticity-how-learning-changes-your-brain/.

Mischel, W., Ebbesen, E. B. and Zeiss, A. R. (1972). Cognitive and attentional mechanisms in delay of gratification, *Journal of Personality and Social Psychology*, 21(2), 204–218.

Mitchell, K. (2012). Ivan Lendl enjoys the crack as unlikely double act take centre stage, *The Guardian* (13 January). Available at: https://www.theguardian.com/sport/2012/jan/13/ivan-lendl-andy-murray-australian-open.

National Institutes of Health (2013). Common Genetic Factors Found in 5 Mental Disorders. Available at: https://www.nih.gov/news-events/nih-research-matters/common-genetic-factors-found-5-mental-disorders.

Pryce-Jones, J. (2012). Ways to be happy and productive at work, *Wall Street Journal* (25 November). Available at: http://blogs.wsj.com/source/2012/11/25/five-ways-to-be-happy-and-productive-at-work/.

Public Health England (2014). *The Link Between Pupil Health and Wellbeing and Attainment: A Briefing for Head Teachers, Governors and Staff in Education Settings* (London: Public Health England).

Reivich, K. and Shatté, A. (2003). *The Resilience Factor: 7 Keys to Finding Your Inner Strength and Overcoming Life's Hurdles* (New York: Broadway Books).

Rheinberg, F., Vollmeyer, R. and Rollett, W. (2005). Motivation and action in self-regulated learning. In M. Boekaerts, P. Pintrich and M. Zeidner (eds), *Handbook of Self-Regulation: Theory, Research and Application* (San Diego, CA: Academic Press), pp. 503–509.

Rosenthal, R. and Jacobson, L. (1968). *Pygmalion in the Classroom: Teacher Expectation and Pupils' Intellectual Development* (New York: Holt, Rinehart and Winston).

Rosete, D. and Ciarrochi, J. (2005). Emotional intelligence and its relationship to workplace performance outcomes of leadership effectiveness, *Leadership and Organization Development Journal*, 26, 388–399.

Seligman, M. (2006). *Learned Optimism: How to Change Your Mind and Your Life* (New York: Vintage Books).

Seligman, M., Ernst, R., Gillham, J., Reivich, K. and Linkins, M. (2009). Positive education: positive psychology and classroom interventions, *Oxford Review of Education*, 35(3), 293–311.

Simons, D. J. and Chabris, C. F. (1999). Gorillas in our midst: sustained inattentional blindness for dynamic events, *Perception*, 28(9), 1059–1074.

Swainston, T. (2012). *Coaching for Change: Creating a Self-Development Culture* (London: Optimus Education).

Swainston, T. (2012). *The 7Cs of Leadership Success: Unlock Your Inner Potential and Become A Great Leader* (Bloomington, IN: AuthorHouse).

Sweeney, T. (1989). *Adlerian Counseling* (1st edn) (Muncie, IN: Accelerated Development).

Syed, M. (2011). The words that could unlock your child, *BBC News* (19 April). Available at: http://www.bbc.co.uk/news/magazine-13128701.

Tasman, A., Kay, J., Lieberman, J. A., First, M. B. and Riba, M. (eds) (2015). *Psychiatry*, 2 vols (4th rev. edn) (Chichester: Wiley-Blackwell).

Thoreau, H. D. (1906). The Journal of Henry David Thoreau. In B. Torrey (ed.), *The Writings of Henry David Thoreau: Vol. XIII* (Boston, MA: Houghton Mifflin).

Bibliography

Veenman, M., Van Hout-Wolters, B. and Afflerbach, P. (2006). Metacognition and learning: conceptual and methodological considerations, *Metacognition and Learning*, 1(1), 3–14.

Wilson, D. with Conyers, M. (2015). Positive brains are smarter brains, *Edutopia* (9 December). Available at: http://www.edutopia.org/blog/positive-brains-are-smarter-brains-donna-wilson-marcus-conyers.

The A Level Mindset

40 activities for transforming student commitment, motivation and productivity

Steve Oakes and Martin Griffin

The A Level Mindset

40 activities for transforming student commitment, motivation and productivity

Steve Oakes and Martin Griffin

ISBN: 978-178583024-2

In *The A Level Mindset*, Steve Oakes and Martin Griffin share the secrets of coaching students to develop the characteristics, habits and mindsets which will help them realise their potential. Those students who make real and sustained progress at A level aren't necessarily the ones with superb GCSEs. Some students leap from average results aged 16 to outstanding results aged 18. Others seem to hit a ceiling. But why?

It was in trying to answer this question that the VESPA system emerged. Steve and Martin have cut through the noise surrounding character development and identified five key characteristics that all students need to be successful: vision, effort, systems, practice and attitude. These characteristics beat cognition hands down. Successful students approach their studies with the right behaviours, skills and attitudes: they understand how to learn and revise effectively, they're determined and organised, they give more discretionary effort and they get top results. Success at A level is a result of character, not intelligence.

The A Level Mindset Student Workbook offers students a structured way to work through the 40 activities in *The A Level Mindset*. Sold in packs of 25. ISBN: 978-178583079-2.

Puffed Out
The Three Little Pigs' Guide to a Growth Mindset
Will Hussey and Barry Hymer

ISBN: 978-178583117-1

Puffed Out: The Three Little Pigs' Guide to a Growth Mindset by Will Hussey and Barry Hymer is a comprehensive catalyst for cultivating a growth mindset. Schools increasingly value grit, determination, resilience and adaptability as being key to deep learning. But how do you put these values into practice? This innovative approach starts by getting learners to think about a seemingly familiar story in a radically different and creative way.

This book might seem to be about the three little pigs, but the pigs are just the focus of its real purpose, which is to challenge and encourage learners to immerse themselves in thinking between, above, below, around and beyond the tale's unexplored blind-spots. Crammed full of activities and diverse open-ended questions, there's plenty to ponder over, and if they require a nudge or two in the right direction, they'll find them – although the direction they take depends on which way they're looking at it. Prompts and responses abound, although it's not always clear which is which; questions can be answered and answers should be questioned.

Suitable for primary and lower secondary teachers.

Stretch and Challenge for All
Practical Resources for Getting the Best Out of Every Student
Torsten Payne

ISBN: 978-178583159-1

Stretch and Challenge for All: Practical Resources for Getting the Best Out of Every Student by Torsten Payne is packed with activities to get the most out of learners in any lesson. If you have a class of 30 students, how can you differentiate so that every learner is challenged appropriately? These tried-and-tested techniques are designed to engage and stretch all pupils, including the most able, and can be used with mixed ability groups in any key stage or subject lesson. If you are looking for ideas which will enthuse all students and develop their understanding and thinking skills, this is the book for you.

The activities can be used at any stage of the lesson and include ideas for: interactive aims, stimulating starters, challenging questions, writing strategies to stretch the student, showing the progress, plenaries and revision, and mastering metacognition. Discover practical strategies to add challenge to all types of lesson, across all subjects and key stages.

Suitable for all teachers.